ADVANCED PRAISE FOR *GHOST TOWN ODES*:

"When I started reading Matt Schumacher's poems, I had no idea I'd be getting a lesson in Pacific Northwest history. But what a lesson! From the farcical gold mine at Bourne, Oregon, in the 1800s, to the native villages clustered along the Columbia riverbank before enormous dams built during the last century flooded Celilo Falls, Matt writes with great sensitivity and knowledge of his subjects. Vivid images fuel the imagination with a longing for what once was. Matt knows his history and his poems reflect his research. The collection goes superbly on: There are "The Deep Creek Yuan Gui Speak their Grievance," "Ballad of a Basque Sheepherder," and many more, all poignant and delightful, not just for those who appreciate well-written poetry, but also for those who want to learn more about the region's colorful—and too often tragic—history."

—R. GREGORY NOKES, author of *Massacred for Gold:*
The Chinese in Hells Canyon and *Breaking Chains: Slavery on Trial*
in the Oregon Territory

'In the tradition of *Odas Elementales*, the poems in Matt Schumacher's *Ghost Town Odes* resonate with insight and a sensory exuberance that revels in natural complexity and this chance we have to live on Earth. Sandwiched between lively and visionary pieces grounded in Schumacher's life, the ghost odes are a mythohistorical motherlode in which narrative lyricism serves as a medium for settlers and tribespeople whose presence can be said to still reside in the West (particularly Oregon). In the odes, places come to life, seen through eyes of former inhabitants who, conjured up, share perspectives and values they held to. Throughout this collection is an indomitable generosity of spirit accompanied by considerable associative facility that communicates intrinsic importance of human and ecological realities."

—JAMES GRABILL, author of *Sea Level Nerve (Book One)*
and *Sea Level Nerve (Book Two)*

"With a title like *Ghost Town Odes*, a reader might expect Matt Schumacher's latest poetry collection to be an extended consideration of loss: lost places, lost lives, lost stories and histories. To be sure, that sort of loss is tallied here. Cemeteries live on sans their antecedent towns, and even the postscripts are ghosts, forgotten or unwritten. But in all this necessary tallying, there's more than straight-line elegy. There's celebration, too, of the things we too often ignore. Here, the backdrops are brought into the foreground; the heretofore unheard voices of the Pacific Northwest's so-called Manifest Destiny are heard. Most of all, the gray-green flora and fauna of lower Cascadia—where so many of these poems are set, where all this history happened, or was dreamed—shines in a lapidary, liquid light that puts all our new-fangled neon to shame."

—TJ BEITELMAN, author of *Americana*
and *Communion: Stories*

"In this rich and remarkably inclusive collection, Matt Schumacher renders forgotten towns un-forgotten. With vivid imagery and music, he re-members, he re-embodies them onto pages of a poetic atlas. Here, a grateful reader also discovers tales about saloons and cemeteries, Great Plains buffalo and a pot-bellied pig, wild huckleberries and the bits of wedding cake fed to a deer. In one of the book's four sections, Schumacher offers epistolary persona poems that give a panoply of candid and often wrenching histories, laments, confessions, and revelations. The chronological and geographical scope of this collection is impressive. *Ghost Town Odes* holds an ambitious and admirable trove of poems."

—PAULANN PETERSEN, Oregon Poet Laureate Emerita,
and author of *The Voluptuary* and *Understory*

Ghost Town Odes

REDBAT
BOOKS
PACIFIC
NORTHWEST
WRITERS
SERIES

Ghost Town Odes

MATT SCHUMACHER

redbat
books

redbat books
2016

Printed in the United States of America

First Trade Paperback Edition: October 2016

ISBN 978-0-9971549-2-4
Library of Congress Control Number: 2016954576

Published by
redbat books
2901 Gekeler Lane
La Grande, OR 97850
www.redbatbooks.com

Text set in Adobe Jenson Pro and Bountiful

Cover Photo: "Tinder Box" by David M. Cobb
Book design by Kristin Summers, redbat design | www.redbatdesign.com

For Kaley and the Animals

Table of Contents

Oregon Idylls

Autumn Idyll 3

Forest Road 1819: Rhododendron, Oregon 5

Ode to the Vaux's Swifts at Chapman Elementary School 6

First Snow in the Mt. Hood National Forest 8

Crater Lake Ode 9

In Praise of Slowing Down 10

The Cloud Hour 11

Keeping It Weird 13

Bridal Veil... 15

Mt. Tabor Epithalamium.. 16

Please Don't Pick Up the Papayas.................................... 19

Eden 21

Paean to a Parkdale Pear... 23

Picking Blackberries Outside the Sandy DMV................. 24

Huckleberrying... 26

Ghost Town Odes

Snowstorms of Cornucopia 29

Ballad of a Basque Sheepherder: Shaniko, Oregon............ 31

The Deep Creek Yuan Gui Speak their Grievance:
    Hells Canyon 33

World Renewal Ceremony: Celilo Falls, Oregon 35

Bayocean... 37

It's No Eldorado... 39

What Cheer 40

Running on Fumes at Wilson Station and Cafe:
    Kent, Oregon 41

Roosevelt 43

Why the Badlands Look So Bad 45

You've Looked Better 47

Elmer McCurdy Visits Malheur City, Oregon 48

Rhyolite 51

Greenhorn 52

Played out at the Hard Case 53

Recipe 54

Three Cemeteries Without Towns 56

Tule Lake 58

Idiotville 59

Lost Letters from the West

Sitting Bull Writes to Crowfoot from Buffalo Bill's
Wild West Show: New York, 1885 63

Dr. W. T. Phy Tells Why Hot Lake Hotel is Haunted:
Hot Lake, Oregon 66

Ghost Town Requests Her Majesty's Presence
Singing Country Western Song: Antelope, Oregon 68

F. Wallace White Recites his Swindler's Soliloquy:
Bourne, Oregon 70

The Bard Teleported to the Old West:
Shakespeare, New Mexico 72

Lost Letter from Matilda Sager 74

Letter to James Isabell 77

Henry Deadmond 78

Henry Griffin Tells the Truth About the
Lost Blue Bucket Mine: Auburn, Oregon 79

Fueled by a Case of Whiskey and a Stubborn Mule,
the Notorious James Long Founds Granite, Oregon 81

Dissatisfied Tourist Complains: Santa Claus, Arizona 83

The Gang Moves Back to the Hotel: Shaniko, Oregon................. 85

Driving Past Medical Springs 87

Joe Bush, Phantom Dredgemaster, Spirits You Away:
    Sumpter, Oregon.. 89

Vanport.. 91

A Final Duel Between Big Bill and the Cowboy Detective:
    Tiger Hotel Lobby, Burke, Idaho....................................... 92

Chief Joseph Visits Joseph the Elder's Grave:
    Joseph, Oregon 95

Pastoral with Bestiary

Dear Sulcata Tortoise... 101

For the Vanished Herds of Great Plains Buffalo....................... 102

Horseheaven 103

The Subtle Art of Smuggling a Young
    Vietnamese Pot-Bellied Pig to Oregon 104

Big Guy's... 107

Kindness.. 108

Yokum Ridge 109

Missed Photos 110

Angel's Rest... 112

Nocturne 113

Reverie 115

Paean to the Snake River Grade.. 116

Ape Cave 118

Progress 120

Life as a Cloud in the Blue Mountains....................................... 121

Oregon Idylls

Autumn Idyll

This October morning, my wife admired
a crimson maple on Albina,
scattering the genius of its foliage.
I'd love to have a dress that color,
but that's impossible, she replied,
as if the tree had asked her
if she'd like to try on every leaf.
But suppose we became so acquainted
with the sun and shade today that they emblazoned
tones too bold for any wardrobe,
imbued fabric with pure revery,
unveiled sleeves that exceed the zeal
of shooting stars, stitches which dart
and dive, as alive as sparrows?
What if, just this once, autumn meant
nothing ever had to die again
and this sun the hue of fading yarrow
showed us lost yellows of stalk and husk,
let us borrow unknown oaken browns,
lit by bonfire and pumpkin,
all of it, the entire history
of autumn, knit into a dress
possessed by negligible senescence,
unzipped by psithurisms?
Wearing it's a chill wind which rescinds
lists of long, hot augusts from the skin.
Trim and hem embed last reds,
deciduous bodice of breathing, gold-edged thread,
pleated with last summer's green,
splashed with purple aster and chrysanthemum.

Migrating flights of Monarch butterflies woven in
with blue sky, lunar eclipse.
A dress that sets the feet down deep as roots,
unharmed by frost, safely within earth all winter long.
Clothed in fall's tresses,
bare arms become manifold branches.
They'd unfold choirs, breaking into April song.

Forest Road 1819:
Rhododendron, Oregon

This road, so yellow-gold with maple leaves,
should lead to an undiscovered country,
a land of permanently crisp, chill air
and sunlit, azure sky, where you and I
can wander anywhere and feel welcome.
These fallen leaves larger than our hands
should be worth far more than money somewhere.
They've paved this forest road, as if it leads
to such a place. Maybe we're already there.
For now is the time of year that orchestras
unfold inside these trees, violin and woodwind,
until forests echo with bright colors
and crimson music. Listen to a symphony old
as the world, falling differently on every eye and ear,
as light turns roads gold, or weeps red leaves.
Listen to its final concert, a music we can see and hear,
before the world turns white with the first snow.

Ode to The Vaux's Swifts
at Chapman Elementary School

While in the wild they'd hide for the night within a snag,
one colony in 1982 decided
they'd roost in the cement chimney
of a Northwest Portland elementary school,

and, thirty years later, on September nights
just before sunset, crowds gather to watch
up to 40,000 swifts tuck themselves into a smokestack.
Each year the school won't use the flue until they fly back

to the Yucatan. I'm here tonight, craning my neck,
standing and squinting with the rest
in a blocked-off street, just in time
to see the first few swifts drift out.

There they are, a child declares. Then more
and more, a soaring, shapeshifting aviary, lifts the crowd's eyes,
affecting momentary patterns so exact
there must be some algorithmic pact, or fractals they enact,

they may be a shadowplay of quintessential shapes
that hold together our world, that keep night and day in place.
These geometries they fracture when they disband, are remade,
evanescent, as they fly to heights beyond the eye's capacity.

It's pure ritual we can't fully understand,
can't fully be part of. We have no idea
what these small birds must feel like up there,
though they appear to immensely enjoy themselves.

But I wish all my friends and family were here, intact,
my entire scattered flock, my mother, who adored birds, especially.
She'd love these dives and ascents,
their storm forming an acrobatic vortex.

Dark stars practicing their art, darting across the sky,
each swift retires with its small taste of evening,
bits of the night, building nightfall like a nest.
Here they are again, steering us toward

a new way to view sunset, gliding with the dying light
held in the iridescences of their feathers,
the clouds turning pink, the day fading,
the hillside of oohs and ahs, and finally, applause,

as the funnels slowly unfold one by one,
revolving until the last swift fits safely in.
Each wing finds its place folded among thousands.
Each bird hatched from a tiny cup of twigs,

one of three eggs in a mountain crevice in a cliff,
to survive so many nights. What were the odds
any one of them would live? This is why mothers
pull covers up tight to hide their children's chins—

The wilds of night encircle us completely,
frighten with so many eyes, a spire in a primeval cavern
looking down like a feathered god
on everything that's ever lived.

First Snow in the Mt. Hood National Forest

The power's out
in Rhododendron, Oregon, again.
The cabin dim.
Overnight, a soft white
decides to quietly
drape the junipers and pines,
until some trees seem completely
composed of snow.
Drowsily, our eyes
find the edges
of the blinding world.
The sun seems to be melting
a world of tall, white trees.
Light's suddenly liquid. Every drop
in this dripping forest
sparkles.

Crater Lake Ode

You'll never view blue this unearthly
unless you peruse its depths in person.
Such blue mystifies the eye
from rhapsodizing iris
to stupefied pupil,
immerses tourist
and glowing oceanographer.
No one can map the place
Crater Lake's blue takes you.
Shades this deep must be trapped
for centuries inside collapse,
in shadows cast by blown volcano dome,
and slowly released each season,
through melting ice and blizzards
that encastle Wizard Island's pine spires,
as if, with open eye,
the earth were dreaming.

In Praise of Slowing Down

How worthwhile to slow down
and know the alpenglow,

as elk cross Lolo Pass
just past our headlights

into twilight shadows.
Slow down and you

might find wild blackberries,
their swollen ripe beads glistening

beneath leaves and thorns,
find sweet, soft seeds adorn

the gravel road to Zigzag Mountain.
Since slowness slips us glimpses of the deep,

spotted bells of pink, spiked foxgloves,
small steeples which seem suddenly

filled with doves, or thrills us with
the sulphur shelf's yellow-orange frills,

regalia for fallen logs, heretofore unknown
heroes of forest folklore, and frees our sight

to light, butterfly-like, on Lost Lake,
exquisite in the distance between dense trees,

it makes humankind more humane
and mindful. Slow down. Please.

The Cloud Hour

Emerson, it's said, banished his children outside
if they misbehaved at dinnertime,
as part of an unusual punishment:

they were to observe the clouds
for a specified period of time
and, upon returning to the table,

to describe precisely what they'd seen.
There, sadly, the anecdote ends,
which suggests it's best to guess at the results:

children so proud they couldn't possibly sulk,
half-floating in the front door, bubbling over
with dreamy speeches or vaporous fables,

prepared for serious cumulus discussion:
brief treatises titled *fanciful affairs of thin air*,
or despairing soliloquies from lost kings

whose lopsided castles toppled over in pure silence;
blissful tales of mischief from the one puff
who glowingly hides the sunshine,

mimicked howls from bestiaries of fantastical animals,
evolving, then dissolving before our eyes,
introduced as by some grand sleight-of-hand

from some deity or eminent stratospheric magician.
And later, perhaps even the same evening,
the fortunate young Emersons

might well be whistled downstairs to the back door
only to be told stories, willed keepsakes, and offered
fresh popcorn by their father's friend, Henry Thoreau.

Keeping It Weird

As the yellow pickup truck with the pink unicorn sticker
on its passenger side pulls up alongside us
at a gas pump on North Lombard
this bright decal of a fabled beast
might mean the truck contains an enchanted forest ranger,
or that the driver serves as veterinarian
who deals solely with imaginary creatures.
Maybe he has spent his life searching for unicorns
and believes he even glimpsed some on occasion.
Perhaps he travels with prepared lectures on their features.
Speculation such as this is not ridiculous—
keep in mind this conceivably could be
the only pickup truck in the world
bearing a pink unicorn on its side.
But one expects exceptional ideals
in this city, where just earlier today
an aged, bearded landscaper sauntered past,
towing weedwhacker and rakes down the street,
shovel and tools almost overflowing
from his child-sized red wagon—
as if William Carlos Williams' wheelbarrow
had been hijacked by Walt Whitman.
It's rare to stare too hard at anyone here.
The girl hulahooping herself giddy on a grassy island
in the college parking lot is not at all overdoing it.
She could, in fact, become a welcome fixture here.
Her euphoria reminds my wife and me, driving by,
that we never want to leave.
What extraordinary sleight-of-hand
will this city next reveal from up its sleeve?

Tightrope walkers strutting barefoot
across ribbons tied to trees in Kenton Park?
Where else but Western Oregon do people hulahoop
with wild abandon in a parking lot,
without one gyration out of place?
Only in this great, green-hearted state. Only here.

Bridal Veil

Someone names a small town
after a waterfall since
its delicate trail of mist
looks like a bridal veil.
A ghost town's history ensues:
Larch Mountain pine
falls down a log flume to
the disappearing Palmer sawmill.
Lumber boom families
perish due to smallpox
and diphtheria epidemics.
The trust for public land destroys
the last standing buildings,
except for the cemetery,
but thankfully, there's more
to the metaphor: the air wears vapor
like a layered dress.
All is defined by a shining finery of rain,
and a tiny post office rests
by the highway like
a clapboard chapel of true happiness.
Thousands of brides and grooms
briefly stay, in spring and summer,
soon on the way to honeymoons.
They send guests wedding invitations
bearing Bridal Veil's insignia of bliss:
its postmark like a goodbye kiss
from a forgotten town.

Mt. Tabor Epithalamium

Twice a week, we circle a volcano,
our stimuli-mad labrador/springer spaniel's whims
pulling us sideways. Crisscrossing
the footpaths of Mt. Tabor,
my wife and I embark upon a city park
fit for a memorable reign, or more of a forest
where lifelong wanderers feel royal.
Our most awkward twists
and turns crowned by white trillium.
Rhododendrons overloaded
with purple clustered blooms
stand by like ruffled palace guards
as if our every step is necessary
to open each successive flower.
Summer hillsides pour forth green,
spilling golden dandelion hours.
The egalitarian Tabor spring rain maintains
maybe all our travels weren't in vain.
Every visitor, treated to scenery
announcing the downtown skyline,
as well as the Willamette Valley,
may stroll walkways and elaborate grounds,
pause at restroom chateaus
or linger like a proud monarch on tour over reservoirs
whose modest gatehouses
resemble romanesque lakeside castles
somewhere in The Alps in small scale model.

Maybe it's my German ancestry,
but it's clear I'm getting carried away

not just by Tolstoy, our dog named for a Count,
but like Mad King Ludwig II of Bavaria,
my dreams retreating to the Linderhof Venus grotto
or moving to the winter garden on the roof in Munich.
Any worthy, down-to-earth Emperor and Empress Norton
would be sure to survey these serene pools
that fortify their fair city
with drinking water and electricity,
like we tour Tabor's reservoirs twice a week.
And any make-believe queen and king
must feel revered to stroll beneath trees such as these
Atlas Blue Cedar and Sequoia.
The regal should indeed feel insignificant
beneath these Bigleaf Linden
and Portuguese Cherry Laurel.

Maybe, for our short time here, there's heraldry:
Maybe Tabor enthrones those who saunter
its canopied paths. Even the drunk kid
arrested for pissing in the city water supply
like some foolish duke
was a truly abrupt voluptuary
and the couple caught skinnydipping
felt like royalty finally taking a bath for their brief minute.

After all, our carpet's more spectacularly stark
than any emperor's: a blood-red lava river
erupted, flowing from this cinder cone
not long ago, geologically speaking,
incandescent and present right here
beneath our feet and these umbrellas,
deflecting spheres of ice

from today's hailstorm.
Perhaps these bicyclists
like brightly dressed messengers
really are rushing off to share secrets,
deliver wisdom to faraway kingdoms,
and these joggers, loyal subjects,
hurry away to complete crucial imperial duties.
Maybe I should confide in my wife
that, with these white petals
of Umbellularia decorating the road today
like confetti, I have the notion we're
being secretly remarried,
especially on a day like this,
with its blue sky brandishing
ceremoniously huge cumulus clouds,
and this brisk wind, refreshing our spirits
with reminiscences of coastal ocean.
We shouldn't be surprised to see
the 1960 Willys Jeep pull up
with her father, Richard, driving.
Wait one more moment and we may find ourselves all dressed up
and standing alongside Wallowa Lake in late October,
the snow melting on the trees all around us
as it did when we read our vows
and afterward, when we fed wedding cake to deer
in what must have been the only patch
of sunshine anywhere for miles
in the autumn cloudbursts of the mountains.

Please Don't Pick Up the Papayas

The night a papaya escaped our cart
at some unknown location in New Seasons grocery,
that fugitive fruit left us so surprised
we almost questioned our vegetables.
What on earth had happened to that stray papaya?
Maybe, had we paid attention, we could have seen
some guy who craves papayas lose control
of his desires, and grab our papaya,
and dash away greedily hording it,
holding the papaya close to his body
as if it were his long lost child
and looking all around in papaya paranoia.
Alternatively, the papaya, dangling
and jarred by a mango, might have slipped away
through those holes for kids' legs,
then briefly rolled down the aisle
like a somersaulting green baby armadillo.
Perhaps two children stole the papaya
and began an elaborate game
they'd made up, a tropical hide and go seek.
Yes, I can see them now as they sneak the papaya
from one cart to another, without
customers noticing, as they smile.
Hey, what if the papaya simply never
made it into our cart? What if the bright lights
and colors of the produce section
left us delusional with fruit,
like a centerfielder momentarily blinded?
Maybe it is okay to blame
the pummelos for their bright yellows,

to implicate the ruby red grapefruit,
the looming sour of the rhubarb?
It's possible some subconscious part
of us asked who needs a papaya, anyway?
All we need is a small basket
of seedy sweet, glistening blackberries.
Who knows? We might entertain the unlikelihood
that the papaya stood up, stuck out some sort of thumb
and started hitchhiking, and someone else decided

to pick it up, someone who'd needed
to eat a papaya for a long, long time.
This papaya was precisely what
had been missing from their life.
And, from now on, this customer
will remain forever satisfied.

Eden

Why do these dudes who work as grocery produce clerks
often develop crushes on my wife?

One told her she reminded him of Pocahontas.
Another confided a full appreciation for her style:

you always wear the coolest clothes. Yes, she dresses well,
but it might be her smile, which makes things seem right

with the world, as if there's hope for the hungry, a chance
we might be forgiven. It might be the sight of her turns any
      bitterness sweet

as a soft, ripe Hachiya persimmon. Or maybe the red highlights
of her hair remind them of all the sunshine it took to grow

the finest oranges and lemons in all of Florida or California.
She's fine enough to ruffle every head of romaine lettuce.

Her brown eyes big and hot as skillets might fry all the
      potatoes on the spot.
A man might fall as senseless as a Walla Walla sweet onion.

Dates and figs get dark and heavy on their trees, dreaming
of falling into her long, slender fingers.

It could be they feel like they're in Eden
the same way I did when I first watched her eat a pomegranate

or avocado. I remember telling her so.
Who can blame them? One glance at her amidst

all the lush greenery, the ripe fruits and vegetables,
and it's like the world has just begun.

Paean to a Parkdale Pear

I ate an incredible pear yesterday.
It was the ideal, the absolute green fruit
Lorca said must be eaten under the moon,
the otherworldly globe, the handful of duende.
The green skin of a far unexplored planet,
the white of which, like a tiny antarctica,
refreshing and subterranean,
dripping like a secret cavern, gave life
to stalactites and glistening spires
of castles. The first bite restored all
the lush forests on the north side of Mt. Hood.
It was the kind of still life
you could be happily trapped inside forever.
White territory of epiphany.
Bodhissatva of the fruit
Plath entitled *little buddhas*.

Picking Blackberries Outside the Sandy DMV

This is easily the best time I've ever had at the DMV,
which isn't saying much. But hey—
I'm not stuck waiting in a long line
to take a test, or paying eighty bucks
to reinstate my license,
or being told I don't have the right kind of i.d.
by some officious state employee
enjoying bureaucratic rules a bit too much,
or squinting my way through the eyesight test,
then closing half-blinded eyes
while my picture's taken.

Don't tell anyone, but I'm sneakily
picking the finest blackberries I've ever tasted—
plucking giant, exquisitely ripe,
pure exemplars of their species—
right behind the building, and feeling illegal
and a little guilty elation,
because they're completely free
and the people inside, are, no doubt,
suffering the usual misery, fines, and fees,
while I'm voraciously feeding on an invasive species,
braving stiff thorns
and hunter-gathering the himayalan
in the shadow of the modern
department of transportation.

I predict these blackberries
will be cold and magnificently sweet.
Eating them, in fact, I believe my wife and I will feel
like we've surpassed the speed limit of sweetness—
a limit defined suddenly by these blackberries.
Their flavor's pure luxury will far
exceed any ride in a limousine.
We'll eat them after they've chilled
for two days in the refrigerator—
on what may be the hottest day of summer.

They'll be so good I'll be forced to return
to pick more, and people may stare
and think I'm strange, but, for the first time in my life,
I will be grateful for the DMV.

Huckleberrying

At the right altitude in late July,
between needlegrass, lupine, and gooseberry,
you can walk away with bowlfuls
of sweetly sour reddish-purple berries,
swiped, perhaps, from black bear paws,
which might have later harvested their spheres
as dessert after salmon and wild onion.
You can wind up addicted to the criminal thrill
of huckleberrying, not minding the dust,
or reckless, speeding pickup trucks,
and, hurrying to your car with more
than you thought you could carry,
find yourself flying down Fox Road
at twilight, ultimately,
your mouth stained the same shade
as the darkening sunset.

Ghost Town Odes

This is the final resting place of engines,
farm equipment, and that rare, never more than
occasional man. Population:
17. Altitude: unknown. For no
good reason you can guess, the woman
in the local store is kind. Old steam trains
have been rusting here so long, you feel
the urge to oil them, to lay new track, to start
the west again.

—RICHARD HUGO, "Silver Star"

Snowstorms of Cornucopia

I bet they kept winter a secret,
or so one might suppose from the proportion of white
exposed in old photos. Perhaps the owners spoke only of gold,
deposits so rich nuggets tumbled out of the mountainside
right into a man's fist, shirt, or boots. Maybe
they warned miners to hurry
up the steep road to the Last Chance,
pocket mine flowing with supine, untold millions.
But no one told how snow would envelop
the porches, the windows, the tallest balconies,
the Hotel Tedrowe streetsign, the roofs
steeply pitched to resist it, even the church steeple,
as if Cornucopia were draped in page after page
of frigid calligraphy, as if the snow
covering everything was some intimate,
handwritten letter the weather was slowly composing.
I doubt anyone bothered to warn the miners about a winter
hardhearted enough to bury the nearby strawberry farm
or to divulge how the snow would slope
from the roof and barricade the doorway
to the saloon, to Brown and Pierce General Store.
Surely no one spoke of the snow's
ominous promises, its glints of blizzard and avalanche,
its flash of slick ice in the dark,
or about its spirituous pact with the wind,
who agrees to design its witcheries
so long as its drifts will sift to the rafters.
Neither, I'm sure, did anyone inform the Cornish miners
about winter's wry irony—
they were forced to tunnel from their door

into the cold morning
and slave away in another man-made cave—
nor did anyone tell them, twirling their pale wives
at Keller Dance Hall, how much they mirrored
the storm outside: gliding by the window
in swallowtails and gown, elegantly snowing.

Ballad of a Basque Sheepherder: Shaniko, Oregon

The foreign land is a land of wolves.
—OLD BASQUE PROVERB

A drunk sheepherder in 1903
could choose between thirteen saloons.
One night a year, I'd sidle through the Pioneer or Silvertooth,
bleat my many demons, *deagru asko*, at the moon,

or throw my money to the wind and visit every one. *Buelta*,
I'd cry, then buy the whole cowtown a round
so they'd be friendly louts. The pay wasn't much anyway.
I'd watch it go like it wasn't mine, blow through it in no time

without even trying. Hell, might as well
whoop it up in the wild wool capitol of the world. No magnate
for the Columbia Southern Railroad
or rich landowner cared about my fate,

could boast a loneliness like mine. *Laga. Bakardade,*
they say in my lost language. After nearly a year of speaking to no one
but my dog and flock on the range, I'd hail the first face.
Strangers in the general store reached for their guns.

I'd talk to practically anyone, knowing full well
they were out to take my money. Too soon, I'd be
muttering *to hell with them all* at each shuttered window.
I'd long to show these petty thieves,

these dirt streets packed with ranch-hands spoiling for a fight,
and that cursing, drunkard Scotsman, Farquahar
McRae, the most honest boss to walk across bluebunch wheatgrass
and fescue, the best I'd ever worked for, what *indarra*,

what sort of fortitude and grit I'm knit from,
but I'd be wobbly as a newborn lamb,
a lost old ram, left behind wanderer from the herd,
sure prey for lynx or mountain lion, gone with the *basajaun*.

My ancestors were tireless stewards of missing and sick lambs.
Here, they say that after a full day, most missing sheep won't return.
Shaniko could give a damn. Who'd look
for a tramp sheepman if I got lost for good?

Never mind that I'd survived the Paulina sheep shooters
who pushed my flock over Sheep Rock, that *Mari*, sacred cow thief,
wild, beautiful deity, she of the red ram and the mountaintop,
brought us back to life. The townsfolk, in disbelief,

will look like they've always known who I am:
the liquor I'll be drinking, the vigilante cattlemen I'll fight.
And this town which had survived smallpox that year
and had buried their dead in unmarked canyon graves knew

I was coming. They'd been waiting like *irelu*
and weren't about to shed a tear over my kind.
To meet my sheeplike social needs I so despise, they'd readied fists
to turn me blue, barkeeps who'd sell me whiskey till I'm broke
        and blind.

They'd like me to guard other men's property for the rest of time.
They'd like me to return next year and spend it all.
They've labeled one jail cell *the palace sleeper*
just for me and the *Gaueko*, right behind city hall.

The Deep Creek Yuan Gui Speak their Grievance: Hells Canyon

To the descendants of six horsethieves
and Wallowa County schoolboys
who massacred us for gold at Deep Creek:
Snake River whitewater can't wash away

what your forefathers have done.
Did you know your dear fathers
cut off our heads so we couldn't tell anyone?

Maynard, Hughes, Evans, dead and gone.
McMillan, LaRue, Canfield, and Vaughan.
So desperate and hateful they cut off our arms,
so angry that we weren't afraid of them,
that we accepted death like the dignified men

they could never be. Deprived of the last sight
of our wives and children. Our 34 tongues
undercurrents in a Hells Canyon tomb,
our skulls and bones still far from home
with no proper burial. We're tired

of the silence. No one thanked us
or came to shake our hands at our shacks and tents
after our labor brought water that saved them.
They poured us no champagne at Promontory Point.
They charged us rent and wouldn't let us own property
white men were given for free. Land of opportunity?

What a joke, cracked at our lack of a chance.

It's hard not to laugh at the ruins, the tombstones, so few
greedy teeth left in their kicked-in smiles.
But how are we to unfurl our 135-mile
furrowed brow, the Eldorado Ditch?
How to unmar sixty acres of scars,

the Ah-Hee diggings? How can our eyes not burn
like miner's candlesticks of Chinese
dying in the Lily White Mine? How not to rave
when you built over our graves in Baker City?

What a strange sense of honor and justice
you have here in America, land where
victims, referred to as foreigners, couldn't press charges,
where the guilty could plead guilty and go free

if they'd killed the Chinese. You daughters and sons
of hungry ghosts, take heed: there were never indemnities.

Get to work now, if truth means anything to you.
You'll need the patience and effort
that we built your railroad with to unearth
all the lies told, to strike the truth's seams,
to find the hidden crimes, the victims silenced
by your falsely written white history.

World Renewal Ceremony: Celilo Village, Oregon

Glooscap promised the people that the beavers in
New Brunswick would never grow that big again.
The beavers will not build a dam so big that it
stops the salmon from getting through.
    —"How Glooscap Created Sugarloaf
            Mountain," Mik'maq tale

Driving by Celilo, I'd like Glooscap
to ride in on the back of his whale
and tell the beavers to get very big like the old days
so they slap down the Dalles Dam with their river-sized tails
until nine miles of whitewater breaks out of jail
to roar over the rocks again,
and the rapids are a conjuration
of a prehuman race of immortals like him,
giants, mountain-makers crawling out of the mist,
great ancestors awakened, the crash of their spoken words
renaming, remaking waterfalls and gorge cliffs,
restored so they're everyone's forevermore:
the healed waters attract millions of glittering chinook,
so many salmon that the seals and sea lions
swim upriver again from the ocean to meet them.
As Klickikat fisherman hover over the river,
levitating on platforms of thin air with dipnets,
they perform a rite which heals the starved, sick, and dead,
and Celilo is an ancient, sacred gathering place again,
it is Tulawat, Cahokia, and Wyam,
so vast a coastline that Chumash and Shasta children

legally stolen and sold into slavery in the 1850s
cross to this shore and can come home free again;
Celilo's so timeless that hundreds of Wiyot
women and children can return to Tulawat
safely from the shore of their suffering
and death on Indian Island,
and Chetco, Takelma, and Coquille driven from their homes
and killed can cross the Rogue River, and greet
their brothers, the Pomo from Clear Lake.
Glooscap subdues the Bureau of White Man's Affairs
and his beavers chew through greed
and spit it out worthless so we all finally live
like nothing has more value than our souls.
So thousands dispossessed, Creeks and Cherokees,
can finally come home from their Trail of Tears.
So all tribes join together at the prayer rock
for the powwow, the big time, in the greatest meeting place
in North America, in existence for 15,000 years.

Bayocean

Only a ghost town tries to welcome passersby
with this kind of *vacancy* sign,
invites you to get lost on Tillamook Spit,
then leads you circuitously through littoral
curves and winding highways to
a billboard advertising its demise.
Why are you surprised there's no one here?
Did you expect a host? Promoter T.B. Potter,
the realtor who built it from mere dream,
would say this bay would one day be
The Atlantic City of the West,
but he died a century ago, in 1916.
His wife claimed he went violently insane,
then disappeared, the same way Bayocean later would
fade into invisibility for good.
Search all day as I did for one trace
of dance hall, for one decaying plank of wood,
one tatter of tent city where investors waited
for their promised homes, one drop leftover
from the great saltwater natatorium,
heated pool suited for opulent electric bathing
next to the Pacific. One puff of the yacht
steam-ferrying the affluent from Portland.
Listen for the bowling alley's crackling pins, for the forgotten
orchestra which played on Wednesday nights.
Little's left except the stifling laughter of the tide.
The proposed amusement park, its every ride,
the whirling life here, all washed away,
like the last house, which vanished in the waves in 1960.
In the end, you only find yourself wishing

you could stand on the grand balcony
of the resort hotel like those tourists
in black and white archival photographs,
overlooking the coast, half-blinded eyes
shaded under sun hats, gazing out at a new century,
but the ocean of the present laughs,
sprays the day in your face, and the sand,
an hourglass as big as a peninsula,
spreads its mosaic of *it can't be*. You can't grasp
the past of this mist-breathed city, can't even
set one foot down
in this town now swallowed by the sea.

It's No Eldorado

You must be stubborn to move here
though your true friends warned you not to.
Don't be surprised if you wake up in jail,
they cautioned, and here you are,
heaped upon the straw floor of this hoosegow.
There's no hurry, though. There's still time
to wait in line for the town's sole outhouse,
to expose your unknown flaws, and joke
you didn't know you had them in you,
to go lawless as a mongrel in Raw Dog, Oregon,
half-blind and fully mad in Gouge Eye, Nevada.
You tried to sleep last night
but some drunken miners rang the town bell
until it cracked. You're far from home
and you know it. No one knows you.
Every time you shut your eyes, you pray
you won't end up windswept,
shot by a stray bullet, and left for dead,
another lost name faded
from a wooden tombstone.

What Cheer

Since my hometown owned a torn down depot,
and a swindler who bilked onion farmers
dealt the town a deathblow
years before my birth;

because I favored old grain elevators
and disused silos piled high inside me
like rockets stuck on earth,
and my heart felt hollow
as a closed post office
hoping to open again sometime,

one July day years ago, without knowing why,
I drove several miles out of my way
to mail a postcard from What Cheer, Iowa.

Slow down for ghosts
like I did if you decide to drive by.
It's good to see hope so weatherbeaten endure,
see it take ramshackle shape as a place
that is the great plains' equivalent to driftwood,
or wonder awhile how a tiny, windblown town
in nowhere's prairie, lost in cornfields
and left behind coal mines,
can be so adrift with forgotten dreams.

Running on Fumes at Wilson Station and Cafe: Kent, Oregon

Two antique Phillips 66 pumps and their drooping hoses
transfix my gaze at a distance,
though closeup, under our noses,
they propose to top us off for 66 ½ cents
per gallon like a punchline to a roadside joke:
This service station serves only dilapidation.
Yes, this true jewel of ruined Americana
and remnant of a faded age, the kind
of half-caved-in oasis faced when nearly out of gas,
presently incites my anxious sigh.
But past motorists fueled up here
for long drives that led to destiny—
sometimes, to the finest times of their lives.
Not long before, jettisoning horse and railroad, they were free
to speed toward receding future dreams in their own automobiles.
So right now, lingering where the last shake shingles peel

off the balding roof's edge,
exposing weathered beams, today Wilson's seems
the precise seam where present parts from past.
Chipped white paint cracks under the hot sun,
but I listen for the ding as our car,
now my father's 1955 Thunderbird, pulls in.
Imagine the wiry man with a grin
shuffling out to wash the windshield:
see the world lose focus, then the squeaky edge,
like consciousness, returns the world and sharpens it again,

sparkling clean. Breathe the overwhelming smell of gasoline.
Before driving away on a summer day, full throttle,
I almost feel the moisture of the chilled bottle,
a cool comfort for the palm,
almost taste the sweet citrus soda
coldly explode in my parched mouth.
Drink Orange Crush refreshing delicious
fizzes its effervescent white sign. Fast as advertised,

the past smiles, waves, and drives away.
Surely some drivers encountered curves they'd never recover from
and turned away from this world and any world above.
And others traded tenderness that meant everything to them,
the way my father always leaned across the seat
to kiss my mother's cheek at that same stop sign at the end
of that same interstate off-ramp,
a gesture she always remembered
of the gentleness and comfort we call love.

Roosevelt

What's left—tram and rafter,
roof beams a few feet beneath green water,
seen when the lake's clear—dared us to stare
into the eyes of lakeside thereafters,
brought thoughts of sunken miner's long lost daughters,
backcountry ballerinas who'd feel the need
to pirouette atop the steeple rippling the surface.
They'd fade in and out like cutthroat trout,

navigating jagged stainglass, their rehearsals
grayish brown with algae, a murky congregation, yet devout.
These gliding girl guides of my mind's eye
repeat histories of Thistle, Utah,
and the Temple of Quechula,
whisper of the Reschensee church bell,
its ring still heard in winter
from the phantom islet tower.
They point to what floated for two decades
after flood and mudslide fast immersed
7000 lives. *Seven years—hardly time*
to bury thirteen in its cemetery,
they'd conclude, and vanish. Fleeting,

drowned town close to Midnight, Idaho,
undone as his suicidal, wounded sons,
you magnify a vision of Theodore's left eye, blind since 1905.
You're the devilfish he never caught in the River of Doubt,
slipping away like a whole wilderness after he dies.
You coated yourself in gold dust like the mythic king
of El Dorado, bathing in a sacred lake—all lies

to show us how fast laws and land
we stand on can be shipwrecked by spring thaw.
Not one cabin could filibust Thunder Mountain mud
or snowmelt whitewater, its legislature's wild rush.
And our guides, where did they skate away to
after their questions surfaced, as if left etched in ice:
what if life survived down there
as Atlantis slid into the midst of Idaho?
What if everyone had just refused to leave,
stubbornly surreal pioneers who learned to breathe
and play the saloon piano
still played today at Yellow Pine school?

Why the Badlands Look So Bad

*…that revelation known as the Dakota Badlands
…gave me an indescribable sense of a mysterious
elsewhere.*
—FRANK LLOYD WRIGHT

Nobody in the old days was glad to see the badlands.
No one thought its dry country a comfort or good omen.
Its vistas showed how much we don't know, and can never imagine,
opened buttes and hoodoos beyond understanding.
It eroded men and made them feel far from home, unfamiliar.
At night, its clay and sandstone looked so unlike the world,
as if the moon were pouring itself over the earth.
In daylight's glare, their parched throats
were afraid to speak, for they were considering the worst,
the ravines of varied sadnesses awaiting them.
Pillars scared horses. Pinnacles split wagon wheels.
The ride across the badlands crumbled stubborn pride.
Ridges opened below into brown and gray rainbows
and gullies carved unsure earth, hurried into graves and ruts.
Cliffs disintegrated, shifting beneath feet.
Spires declared last castles of desolation.
The wind spun webs of sand that widened sky.
Lakota myths said the badlands were oasis
before a northern tribe brought war and spoiled paradise.
The other clans prayed until a storm obliterated the plains.
Waves of earth and fire washed all living things away,
smothered strife like a thief buried to his neck.
The badlands look so bad because

they unfurl what we fear most:
the dust of loss, strangled from us,
the dry and lifeless wreckage of desire.

You've Looked Better

As if the ghost of Broken Hills just jumped out of a windowsill,
looking indisposed, and stared you down
to ask *how are you?* in his threadbare suit,
shot to hell from here to Whiskeytown,
one lone desert poppy ablaze in his lapel.

Like you tried to hide your whiskey from those thirsty ghosts
whose long faces exude gloom in Tombstone,
and those same ghosts stole your horse,
like you walked home with only the coyotes
down forty miles of desert road.

Like you just white knuckled it through Cabbage Hill,
down a steep grade in a blizzard on Deadman Pass,
or Black Bart politely asked, then robbed your stagecoach
as it crawled up a potholed slope in the Siskiyous,
like you've been slowly whittled down by some godawful town,
and you're far from relaxed, half-hacksawed off on Mt. Battle Ax.

Like you'd have to lie about what exactly you've been up to,
like you've almost been hung by your own necktie,
like you haven't seen a blooming yucca in a long while,
like your hide's hung around so long no one would suspect you
of much of anything, especially of looking pretty,
even in Rawhide or Vulture City.

Elmer McCurdy Visits Malheur City, Oregon

If he could still sightsee
from his sideshow makeshift casket,
McCurdy'd do a double take
and make out the name
of a place sold out by fortune
without an ounce of showbiz,
a number of tumbledown dugouts
found out by sun-drenched drought,
hovels arrayed like empty graves,
a town as dead as he is.

If sight were still his,
he'd see these stores and streets gave way to sage;
if blind but sensible to touch, he'd feel the way
there's no shade to be had on a hot day.
Defined by dry and dying junipers, this city
might remind him of his withered history:
His body unclaimed by his mother, Sadie;
his escape from the undertaker
who embalmed him with arsenic
then propped him in the parlor
as *the bandit who wouldn't quit,*
collecting nickels on his tongue
because no one would pay to have him buried.

His Malheur City welcoming committee,
a rusted, half-open mailbox
that grasped its last letter long ago, extends its lost grip
as if in friendship, its handshake skeletal.

Elmer could finally feel at home
with Willow Creek like a dry pile of bones,
at a site where farmer and miner might fight
over the Eldorado Ditch, if the year were still 1902,
because a posse shot him in Pawhuska
after a failed train robbery
to dispute 46 dollars and two
whiskey bottles' worth of loot.

If McCurdy could listen, he'd understand why these parts
may be named after a caved-in tunnel
which entrenched a French miner—
and why no one really knows.
I suspect he'd have it in his head to say
there's no respect for or remembrance of the dead.

He'd turn an ear and nearly hear the old conclude,
nothing can be done, the young sigh, *nothing to do.*

The misery inspired by the '57 grassfire
that darkened 12,000 acres, tired out 200 firemen,
and burned the last buildings to rubble,
left ashes of wooden gravemarkers
restored by far too few headstones with terse epitaphs
might remind him of the times he used too much nitroglycerin,
blew the vault door through a bank in Chautauqua,
blasted the door off the train safe
and melted all the silver he'd hoped to steal.

The stories he'd tell if he could speak
would knock us off our feet, too.
Blow off fingers and toes

like his were posthumously in a windstorm near Mt. Rushmore.
He'd say, *I've had enough now. Please stop right here*
and bury me for good.
But scheming thieves will drag him further west.
An extra in the movies *She Freak* and *Narcotic!*
he'll be featured in the Hollywood Wax Museum,
and finally be found in a California fun house—
in the pitch dark, hanging from the ceiling.
Back in Oklahoma, two feet of cement will be needed
so folks will let him get some rest.

Rhyolite

Fading movie heroes with the blahs travel to Las Vegas
for their last hurrah, but I'd rather die in Rhyolite.
Resting in this no frills basin in the Bullfrog Hills
nearby Death Valley, I won't have to stand in line.

I'd depart from life's last nights silently stargazing,
take in hours of the Perseid meteor shower
through the last standing, shell-shocked walls,
the broken tower of the Cook Bank Building,

and wake to snowcapped Sawtooth Mountain.
Room to lounge abounds on the front stoop
of the mercantile, which commands
that battered dignity reserved for rarest ruins.

All the ways the wind scours the greasewood
say Rhyolite won't conceal what's real.
Its heart of broken concrete calls the bluff
of superficial fluff, excess, dressed-up senselessness,

neon scenes devoid of any meaning.
Its bare charms don't put on airs.
The only roads lead from here to the Funeral Mountains,
to Death Valley, or to test sites for atomic bombs.

I might spend quite awhile with the gila monsters,
or free the secrets from each bottle in the bottle house,
those lost slot machines that cost me nothing.
I'd give odds that this dead town
shows me why I should survive,
convinces me that I should live.

Greenhorn

Two tenderfeet stroll into an Oregon saloon
and ask the barkeep where he'd dig for gold.
One drunk miner escorts them outdoors,
points to a random, distant mountainside.
If I were you, I'd start right there,
he earnestly advises. The miner struts inside alone
and the whole bar laughs out loud.
These greenhorns from out east don't know the joke
and are, of course, far too broke to afford a drink.
They take ridicule for truth, stake a claim,
found a mine, and pluck a motherlode
from earth thought of little worth in 1864,
a quartz gold nugget so big it wouldn't fit
through any roominghouse front door—
bigger than any that miner finds during his lifetime.
Before long, they're buying everyone a round.
That's how Greenhorn, Oregon's smallest town,
population 0 in 2010, was born with fourteen mines,
and how fast the West, for all its lawless flaws,
could deal a far different hand
just when you'd lost so much you thought you were done,
leaving those bold at the right time wildly laughing
like a leprechaun upon a pile of gold,
how fast it could forget your roulette wheel's last spin
and turn scorn to good fortune.

Played Out at the Hard Case

You've stayed so long in Heck and Gone
no one can blame you when you move on
to Bourbon, or turn your brain to mulch
in Whiskey Gulch. Where else in the Old West
could the poor and their next of kin
straggle into again for renewal but a saloon?
You'll get to choose between tangleleg,
coffin varnish, or tarantula juice.
Chances are, you'll be nowhere
near as cool or resourceful as Cochise,
who, turquoise-rich, liked to hide out
in the Dragoon mountains.
Nor could the sad look on your face
match Calamity Jane's
the day she decided once and for all
she was sick and tired of Castle City,
and headed back to Deadwood.
You'd prefer to ride out like her,
without saying goodbye,
but you can't afford to.
A lush in Plush, a ne'er-do-well in Seldom Seen,
your hometown's frowned-upon like some old joke,
but you've no ironies to share that can compare to any known
by the Cheyenne brave named Lame White Man,
dead and scalped by accident at Custer's Last Stand.
You've no job to speak of, yet you need a vacation.
Meanwhile, the barman's taking his time
with your drink, swatting a fly
or two. More than likely
he's seen you before on one too many occasions.

Recipe

Preheat desert excessively. Let it bake all day
like a bad mining camp cook blackens plates.
Knead in human beings eager to succeed.
Prepare desperation and naivete.
Ready dreams of luxury
to meet hardship and death.
Add a teaspoon of hope,
a sprinkle of silver and gold.
Bake in years of severe heat.
Watch the workforce sweat
and rise like temperature's degrees,
slowly climbing until almost free,
then layer by layer, remove good luck.

Wave goodbye to the water supply.
Let liquor and vice try to suffice
as fires torch false storefronts.
Mix whiskey with saloonfuls of fistfights,
gunplay with disreputable ladies.
Build remote homes, bait for apache raids.
Conjure cloudbursts that carry away
the last outhouse. Erode crumbling adobe.
Adorn rotting beams with mesquite thorns.
For irony, leave only tiny jails standing.
Let each tombstone lean
like a history book shook until empty.
Leave the ground too hard for a cemetery.
Don't forget to unlock the rooftop door
marked *winter entrance*, for a way out
during the worst mountain snows,

an escape route for those last souls
who must admit they've finally had it
with this town up to here,
who finally must just call it quits.
Allow room for hollowed-out sound.
Let that emptiness no one will come back to echo.

Three Cemeteries Without Towns

Promise

Promise won't keep
up the pretense of paradise.
No electricity, no lights
and lilacs absolutely criminal abloom,
far too fragrant and pretty for a cemetery
where so many children rest,
never given much of a chance,
lost gravestones with names
like *Teeny Thompson, 1908–1911,*
and six infants, all from the same family.

Sterlingville

Gulches engrave hillsides
like riffles in their flumes.
Abandoned boomtown born in 1854
whose houses, casino, saloons, and stores
all vanished, save for its tombs.
Mary Saltmarsh is still buried here
beside all ten of her children—
none older than ten. Brother and sister
died two years apart, some stillborn.
Others lived one day.
Her gravestone's grateful for each name.
To read each is to hope some joy
relieved her spatterwork from twenty years of grief,
those holes bored inside from hard goodbyes.
Mary's youngest passed during her final year of life.

Mayville

Why such despair prevails on the epitaph
engraved in Mayville's saddest gravestone
won't be told. Whether ruthless truth
or outright lie told out of spite,
it leaves the living feeling more alone:
Henry Beck, 1842–1899
Poorly born
Poorly lived
Poorly died.
And no one cried.

Tule Lake

After the war, when asked where we were born,
children weren't to say *Tule Lake*.
When we did, our teacher frowned as if we'd sworn
or flunked a test. She did her best
pretending it did not exist.

The unspoken lesson was to lose the truth
through falsity and euphemistic list:
protestors and resisters
who fail to swear unqualified allegiance to the U.S.
must be relocated, segregated
in detention due to disloyalty and dissension.

The truth is we were thrown from our homes into a prison,
into the worst conditions, or deported.
Forced to renounce his citizenship,
my father tried to answer unfair questionnaires
but didn't understand English.

Thus, after school, rather than nursery rhymes
or fairy tales, my mother shared camp parables
which taught us to distrust white men:

Listen, she said, taking a deep breath.
In America, you must watch your step.
Hatsuki Watasa, a kind old deaf gentleman
I knew at Topaz, adopted a stray dog.
But he strayed too far one day himself
while trying to free his friend
from barbed wire, and couldn't hear
the orders of the young tower guard,
who shot Hatsuki to death.

Idiotville

Some distance into Dostoevsky's *The Idiot*,
a fop proposes a parlor game:
every player must share a true tale
which reveals their character at its worst.
Readers suspect Myshkin, pure and honest,
will surely be ridiculed and lured
into feeling more out of place on the earth.
But the author abandons the game
after two players' worth of stories fail
to be terribly memorable or incriminating,
because he must get to better things ahead,
as if to say such trifling, petty entertainment
should fascinate us far less than it does.

Along Oregon Route Six in Tillamook State Forest,
a green sign easily missed promotes a town so remote
residents must endure insult. Loggers
salvaged timber from the Tillamook Burn,
a blaze maybe caused by Japanese fire balloons.
You can make or miss the turn, as I did. Either way,
you can pause, but you're caught:
you'll be veering into idiocy.
The famed Russian novelist and little noticed highway sign
both reassure us it's alright to miss Idiotville,
more of a state of mind we should avoid
than a town, whether a hurtful game or cruelty we'll regret.
Why not entirely forget to be idiots,
or at least visit very briefly. According to Fyodor,
if we forgo petty games, it could get more profound.
There'd be fewer wars, and fewer forests would burn down.

Lost Letters from the West

Sitting Bull Writes to Crowfoot from Buffalo Bill's Wild West Show: New York, 1885

Where are the Bright Moons of the June Berry
abloom when you were still a smiling boy?
And the Moons where Deer Shed their Horns?
The Moons when the Wind Tears off Leaves,
the leaves you chased so few years after you were born?
Even the Moons of Sore Eyes, the Hard Moons
have died behind us in the Black Hills, Crowfoot,
and time passes silent as a spruce.

Man Who Never Walked, an old man, wanted to die singing,
fighting the white man on a horse lashed into battle.
If you, my wise child, were here watching, I'd be ashamed.
Bravery's scarce. We're Bill's herd at Dead Buffalo Lake
and his fake battlefield fails to entertain.
His Wild West Show, "The Drama of Civilization,"
lies, civilizes long knives, invents heroes.
A mockery of tomahawk and warcry
almost scalps helpless "settlers"
before vaudeville Bill saves them.
I am the chief who rides once around the ring in paint and feathers
for paid autographs and fifty dollars a week,
encircled by the crowd's hatred.

But you rode in on Bloated Jaw in a dream
a few moons ago and brought hope again.
I wished you were here to see these eastern cities
stun the mind with wonders—hotels, telegrams, phonographs!

These Wasichus leave their children starving on streetcorners.
Last night, I again gave my wages to an orphan, one
who carried a broken guitar. He sang brokenhearted too
for such a young boy, like you do, Crowfoot.
O Great Mystery, after I depart,
show all my sons and daughters home.

Though I've dreamed we'll be killed by our own people,
we need to lead them. I hear your laughter
when Bill's canvas banner's raised behind this show,
like a flag—flat, palefaced painting that imitates
and divides vast sacred space.

What have you heard from the Midnight Strong Hearts?
And Four Robes? Standing Holy? Tell me
the Lakotas are all still alive,
strong and limber as the winds.
Toksa Akhe, Tatanka Iyotake

(*unwritten postscript*)

Crowfoot, forgive my silence,
but on such travels, my world unravels:
Last night, the jeers swelled my visions,

but Lone Dog, who no one could shoot because he was
    with a ghost,
rode into and through the crowd
and what the hecklers saw looked back at them
with a frozen gaze
from the Eden Musee's chamber of horrors wax figures:

Iya followed all of them home
as a starving child who never left their side,
kept them awake all night spinning his spheres
of winter, famine, and disease,
kept them sleepless all night in his tipi of storms,
until they were awakened by the silence of the not yet born,

until they were disturbed by a vanishing baby
in whose wails missing villages are heard.

Dr. W. T. Phy Tells Why the Hot Lake Hotel Is Haunted: Hot Lake, Oregon

That summer, all my favorite patients died,
and the lake smelled like their sad decay.
A tribal leader claimed my pride
had brought bad spirits to the place.
No one else had seen his apparition.
I am a man of science, trial, and fact.
I confess I was obsessed by visions
which disturbed a surgeon who so prizes the exact:
the hotel derelict, in terrible disrepair,
the medical records of long dead patients
spread across the floors upstairs.
Naked bathers paced with an ancient
languor through the ballroom, horrifying
couples, affluent dancing guests.
Sunporch windows showed throes of the dying.
A heaviness stuck on my chest.
The hotel itself came alive as a bad dream.
Gazebos of supposed ghosts. Doors ajar
flew open in the face of screaming teens,
which were the hotel's screams. It was part racing heart
laced with adrenalin. Its many hands lost flashlights,
felt for doors. Past experiments performed
stood upright, made my medical library a fright.
Shadow figures watched me operate. Forlorn,
not the same, I was what science can't explain.
My former wives were versed in my worst fears
and reassembled in the lobby to complain

of my infidelities, then leave in tears.
And Mark, my son, you returned as a child again.
My apologies echoed across the lake.
You wouldn't listen. You played wrong notes
on your saxophone again, the same mistakes
that always made me angry. Every day since floats
on waters that reflect lacrustine trains
unloading passengers at some long vanished depot.
Mist faces breathe beneath the boardwalk in the rain.
This hotel echoes through my stethoscope:
these heartbeats aren't my patients'. Strange breaths stir.
I try to diagnose such ills and I lose hope.
I've caused an affliction I can't cure.
I hear myself cry out as if far away, victim of some brute
sickness, some suffering I can't endure,
crushed under the ruthless, hissing pressure of the truth,
the immeasurably heavy weight of memory.

Ghost Town Requests
Her Majesty's Presence Singing
Country-Western Song:
Antelope, Oregon

Ruthless Sheela, scheming queen of the Rajneeshees,
Wasco County's noose, the truth,
droops from a juniper for you.
Why not fly back from Switzerland and try it on?
A bandana, a dobro, a rhinestone suit with fringe,
and a big beltbuckle that says *BIOTERROR*
await. We'd like to hear you croon
a country-western song soaked with regret,
a fable humbly bemoaning your power binge
from a singer blushed, ashamed of her audacity.
A tune better than any by Tammy Wynette
saying you're truly sorry, not asking for pity,
but admitting you were wrong. How, when
you bought Big Muddy Ranch, moved in
your sannyasins, and renamed Antelope,
you thought it all would fall into your lap.
So sing to us. Come on now. Join in.
Confess the fraud, the wiretaps,
the hit lists, the assassin's failed plans.
The salmonella salads at the Sizzler in the Dalles.
The homeless voters shuttled in
then dumped into surrounding towns.
Tell us you were so paranoid and high on drugs,
so stressed out with guru debts
yet so lassoed by Bhagwan Shree,
you became a power hungry thug.

You'd give hugs, meditate,
then hatefully manipulate.
So Sheela, let your guilty lilt just soar.
Our backup singers will reply right back,
Yes, we know you're not that person anymore.
When your song's over, we'll slide your record
into its jacket of dust, file it with all your other lies.
Antelope will still be here to say we stayed
to celebrate as ninety-three rolls royces,
loaded up on trucks, were hauled away.
We have voices and we're here to say
we may have been a pale shade
like those seven hundred fifty victims
poisoned by your escapades,
the scattered, tattered sage grass
on these hillsides. But we survived.

F. Wallace White Recites his Swindler's Soliloquy: Bourne, Oregon

> *Bourne has been called an open-air closet of skeletons.*
> —BEND BULLETIN

Stunning, isn't it, how presumptuously
the average man takes advantage whenever he can,
how wind invites itself right in
and bares down on a narrow canyon.
Miners who struck gold at Cracker Creek
renamed their camp in 1895
to venerate the owner of the nearby Excelsior mine,
Senator Jonathan Bourne. Son,
that Harvard blueblood's buried in D.C.
and never lived a day in Eastern Oregon.
I was more brash than Bourne's mustache
in black and white photos of the time,
and many fold as bold, as industriously sworn to injustice
as dear Jonathan was bound to uphold the law,
daring like the dark handlebars
bristling to overtake his face and jaw.
My swindles overpowered the hour
when my time came and I was unafraid
to wash away the town's good name.
My name is F. Wallace White, and I moved in,
an opportunistic parasite, spreading, multiplying
lies like disease, publishing my spurious,
embellished version of the news,

boldly printing overestimates of the overflowing gold,
the fake profits of the slowing North Pole mine.
My schemes fleeced many an investor out east
and overseas. My genius was the ease:
the postmaster sorted out my fortune.
I didn't pan or dig an inch. I didn't flinch
but sank my pickaxe fast into these stupid dupes.
I paid thugs to brandish shotguns outside our mines
to assure buyers dreamed of richer ore.
Who'd miss the fun of spilling all their fool
New York and London lucre? Certainly not I.
I built a rustic mansion on the hill
with a rose and white quartz fireplace to rival any luxury.
Its grand staircases arose from my mail fraud proceeds.
I may have lied, but you all need to rake these tailings:
wind, water, human frailty and failing kill.
They're the scoundrels who erode. I am gold.
I breathed the good life into these backwoods,
a shrewd tycoon who cleared out years ago.
And your beloved senator has died.
Bourne, Oregon, you ruined boardinghouse, goodbye.

The Bard Teleported to the Old West: Shakespeare, New Mexico

> *The very rats instinctively had quit it.*
> —SHAKESPEARE, *THE TEMPEST*

Its Elizabethan namesake would be proud.
"I like how this Shakespeare gets around
to killing everyone who stays," he'd say,
fast acquainted with the parlance
of the day and age. "It leaves scenes clean
as you like it in my plays. It does away with
the dramatis personae so they'll need a scribe
to list the tragedies. Its idea of historic's
busy gravediggers burying poor Yoricks.
It trades brave swordplay, surreptitious poison,
for shotguns' bold, dramatic noise, undoing men
who soil their chaps. For boys as cruel as a high noon duel.
For levity, a town of fools who'll fall in fatal traps.
I'm sold on its adobe homes: life fit with tiny windows
fast boarded up to banish woes,
make-shift curtains flirting with a tragic act.
I like shrinking kings. It likes gunslingers:
Billy the Kid, sunk in at Stinking Springs.
Its plot fast as a gunshot.
Brawls hurl ranch-hands
into walls built thick to halt Comanches.
Bad deeds breed ruins. Lost breaths
of innocents who won't return,

ambushed by old west Iagos and Macbeths,
let vengeful spectres lurk.
It leaves behind broken hearts,
but never any silver. That's human work.
It likes villains named William:
Russian Bill, Billy Grounds, Curly Bill, Billy the Kid.
If I were still alive, I'd sign on as sidekick.
We'd do more than outlaws ever did.
I'd write soliloquies its bored drunks would applaud.
They'd pause from shooting flies, bulletholing
saloon walls, to spout philosophy or pray to God.
Horse thieves, too entertained to gallop astray,
could reach bottom in *A Midsummer's Night's Dream*
and never meet a single vigilante. Train-robbers
would still flash, recast as lightning-fast stagehands.
If shows sold out, maybe we'd save hanged men
like Black Jack Ketchum from the gallows,
broaden ways to spare poor players' breaths
upon those scaffolds sheriffs of the West demand.

Lost Letter from Matilda Sager

My dear cousin Henry:
you bear my restless father's name
and appear to also share his daring.
That Henry died on the wagon train to Oregon.
His last breaths inquired how I, a child, would survive,
urged us seven to be brave. In a few more days,
before I could rightly cry or pray, I was an orphan,
burying my mother in a bedsheet in a shallow grave.
But if you must try to fly from a perfectly good nest
and follow your lonesome soul west,
may I suggest it's best not to trust:
Better never turn your back
on these shameless rakes and rattlesnakes
that call themselves human beings.
I've seen cruelty you don't forget:
they'll kill orphan children for a thrill or bet,
for no reason save they'll get away with it.
You're never sure you're not keeping company
with murderers. Blink and kind mothers
slur and curse, turned to bloodthirsty drunks,
lifting little sons and daughters on their shoulders
to see the worst hangings. Good fathers like you
are marked men. They'll hurt the kindest first here, Henry.
Cayuse brought camas then massacred
my missionary stepkin, Marcus and Narcissa.
And my father-in-law, Daniel Delaney,
was slain late one cold night
by his old friend, George Beale.

Given the chance, Henry, there's no end
to what con men will pretend,
what people will steal. That crooked saloonkeeper,
Beale, knew Daniel hated banks
and hid considerable sums in his house.
He blackmailed George Baker, the butcher,
loosened his wits with whiskey,
and loaned him a shotgun
in the hope he wouldn't have to do any killing.
They painted their faces with lampblack
to appeal to Daniel, who showed kindness
to those frowned on by sundowner laws.
Pretending to be lost, they begged
for help to lure him out.

Then Baker shot Daniel until he begged.
Beale finished with his pistol. He shot Little Jack,
his servant boy, and his dog, just in case.

Little Jack survived to testify, but the judge ruled
that a young, half-black boy could not understand
the consequences of his testimony. The court
unanimously agreed the two were guilty anyway.

Hanging day in Salem came
at the scaffold beneath oak trees.
Baker spoke, hoping to spare his wife and children
future suffering. Beale wore white stockings
and read a speech, as well as the psalms,
flashed his silver crucifix, threw his bible to the crowd,
hugged the sheriff like his best friend.

Deputies tied the murderers' legs together.
The gallows' trapdoor dropped.
Their rope came to an end:
Though the noose snapped Beale's jugular,
his neck didn't break. He strangled to death,
swinging for twenty minutes,
ruining his new clothes, his blood
spraying the crowd.

In these kinds of situations, Henry, no one wins.
Thank goodness Chamberlain
made hangings private in 1903.
The cheering and carousing thereafter
was a loud, fiendish scene.
You'd best be ready for some wild country.
If you're headed west, Henry, I suppose
no cautionary tale can stop you. You won't listen to me.
May heaven leave you one step ahead of the fever
and the hanging tree, stave off pain and thievery,
steer you clear of the skilled villains out here.
May you find better friends than George Beale,
better friends than I ever have. Knock on our door
if you need anything. God bless,
Henry. Love, Matilda Jane

Letter to James Isabell

April 16th, 1865

Dear Sir,

I have received your letter regarding the death of your brother, Crawford. I'm convinced that you're the proper one to take charge of your brother's effects. In accordance with your instructions, I have sent the articles and money by express to your address.

You may think the charges large, but they're not, all things considered. We had to travel 160 miles from the settlements into the Indian Country and recover the murderer on our truck. We found the dead bodies
*   and buried them*
the best we could without any coffins. They had been dead fifteen days when we found them. I am very stout-hearted but let me tell you
*   when I came*
to search those bodies and lift them about, it was the hardest trial
*   I have ever had.*
The murderer was named Henry Deadmond. From the best information I have, Deadmond stole one thousand dollars from your brother and about the same from Mr. Meeks. None of that money has been recovered. Deadmond had two thousand dollars when he left home for the valley. He had but five dollars when arrested.

I have a revolver that belongs to your brother and there is a horse in this County that belongs to him also. Please write and let me know what you want done with them.

Yours as ever,

Jesse Cox

Henry Deadmond

After the first hanging in Wasco County, Oregon, in 1865

Indian gunfire tore off half of Henry Deadmond's jaw.
Maybe that made him mean enough to really break the law,
so mean he had to shoot poor George Meek in the head
at Willow Creek, and fill Crawford Isabell, at the campfire nearby,
    with lead
for Henry wanted all Meek's money to himself.
Henry never found the thousand Crawford had hidden in his belt.

Henry too coldly told how thieves had killed both in a letter
    he wrote.
Sheriff White in The Dalles bought Henry a black coat
and a pair of white gloves to wear on the gallows.
Henry's prayer lasted too long. He said *goodbye to all. How*
far will I fall? he asked. *Will my feet touch the ground?*
The sheriff softly answered, *no,* and pulled the black cap down.

The trapdoor snapped. But Henry's neck didn't break.
The crowd of a thousand wondered how long it would take:
Eighteen minutes. 150 women and children watched.
    Did they scream?
Did they stay for it all? Did they cry at the scene?
Did any walk away shamed? Were they short of breath?
The state strangled Henry Deadmond to death.

Henry Griffin Tells The Truth About the Lost Blue Bucket Mine: Auburn, Oregon

A mine is a hole in the ground owned by a liar.
—MARK TWAIN (POSSIBLY ANONYMOUS)

If you weren't yet dead, and hated
your job in those days, you could roam the West
like you deserved respect, making ridiculous claims,
even making up your own name, if you carried
a memorable story and a shotgun.
Auburn began when a charlatan named Adams
tried to guide my friend George and me
who'd bought him too many drinks
and piled our hopes upon his tall tales of gold
in Portland. This huckster swore he'd show us
and a party of sixty-eight more
straight to the fabled Blue Bucket Mine.
On the way, Adams admitted he'd lied:
he'd never been there before. He had no idea
where on God's earth we were,
much less where we'd strike gold.
Right when we gave up, not far away,
the motherlode showed up and said hello,
three feet down a Blue Canyon prospect hole.
What a vacuum. It drew thousands to Burnt River,
swallowed folk from Walla Walla and The Dalles,
names and faces from places faraway I can't pronounce.
A three foot hole started the gold rush, gave birth

to Oregon's most populous town,
6000 strong with whipsaws. Can you believe every
hellraiser there would disappear in four years,
their scrapped empty cabins simply kindling?
All that's left here's a cemetery. Go ahead
and stare, if you care to, at that grave marker
where some wiseacre misspelled my name.
I'm buried by my wife and boy of three.
They passed in that worst summer I'd ever seen.
As the first here and the last to leave, I deserved better.
I came all the way from Maine to stake my claim
and never gave up on this town. It's nothing now,
but in its brief heyday, before we bled foothill and gulch
of the last gold, it dealt unpredictable fates
and fortunes mercurial. It spread like outlaws
where there's no sheriff to be found,
like wildfires in a stiff wind.
It dealt a belt of wealth or a winter
which wore hope down below zero.
Depending on the dance of circumstance,
the dice roll of an instant, a gambler could stand up
as Spanish Tom, desperado who'd stabbed two men
over a card game, chased down by a lynch mob,
or as that shameless liar named John Adams
Auburn turned into a lucky hero.

Fueled by a Case of Whiskey and a Stubborn Mule, The Notorious James Long Founds Granite, Oregon

It's fit for written rule: one favorable unlikelihood
meant restless settlers tried to settle down for good.

Say a stranger's legendary generosity
overflows the Oregon Coast:
a traveler delivers on his boast
that everyone will drink free whiskey this afternoon,
fast taps a flat keg, lets it flow.
Those whereabouts become known as Whiskey Run
because of gushing bourbon, glittering in the sun,
and a nameless stranger's need to prove his word,
but also because miners ran for miles
with washbasins, skillets, pots and pans,
whatever they could grab to trap
the free and flowing multitudes.

Granite sprung likewise from whiskey and luck
when I fell off my mule, stuck in the mud.
As I unstrapped a case of busthead,
lightening my pack to extricate the beast,
Old Blue lifted one filthy hoof as if to kick me dead
through a roof. Gold dust smothered
muck to the horseshoe. Jehoshaphat's
jumping ghost! This shining sight excited all my lust.
Five thousand joined in, boom or bust.
Granite's built as fast as humanly possible.

Those stories of how I'd shoot anyone
who voted for Lincoln? They were all true.

Here in your fancy twenty-first century,
Tourists shoot Granite with cameras
while it sits on its hill with one hell of a view.
Whiskey, painkiller, volatile mother of the gold rush town,
went by many names in my day. You might
try a stirrup cup of Barb Wire. Wild Mare's Milk. White Eye.
Mormon Tea, or Family Disturbance. Quite a list.
In your age, it's distilled instead of swilled.

The lodge's slogan these days says it all:
Desolation at its best. Crane Flats elk
still emerge chestnut brown from dawn each fall,
with coats aglow, then vanish into meadow mist.

Dissatisfied Tourist Complains: Santa Claus, Arizona

Big Nina Talbot weighed three hundred pounds—
plenty of real estate already under her belt,
but that wasn't enough. She bit off more
than she thought when she bought
this godforsaken plot
and helped herself to desolation.
Baiting her tourist trap
with decorated ornate A frame buildings
painted like peppermint candies,
she sold kids dusty Santa Claus
with her Cinderella doll house,
miniature pink train,
and Christmas Tree Inn restaurant.
She believed children would beg
to see Santa Claus all year round, and they did.
Well, their parents just stared out
at all that sand and cactus.
Could you imagine taking your kid
to see Santa Claus every day of the year?
There'd be a true nightmare
with no place to escape.
Any fool could plainly see
there were no reindeer
in the Mojave Desert.
Decor adorable as a scorpion.
Not one shriveled elf in the agave.
Someone needed to convince Nina
it's not on anyone's wish list

to live nowhere and play make believe.
People would stop by to see Santa Claus,
then leave.

The Gang Moves Back to the Hotel: Shaniko, Oregon

No one there made fun of us or stared,
but the state moved us to a nursing home, where we died.
Maybe space and time decided they don't care.
We earned the right to come back when we like.
No tourists or billionaires will bother us
because the hotel's closed. We slowly wake,
stretching our legs over the watertower's edge,
like doves taking Bakeoven in from above.
Down forgotten stairs no longer there
on a morning filled with all kinds of blue sky,
quiet enough to not trouble a soul.
Days like today it doesn't matter that we're dead.
We have the hotel all to ourselves.
I'm Charley Franks, beekeeper, potato peeler,
but don't tell me to peel vegetables or tend bees—
we're retirees for eternity, heaven knows.
That's Gene Kent, president of folding clothes.
Howard Lane's our sheriff with the paper star,
and Melton Sawyer thinks he's in charge
of smoking up the place.
Don't give that ghost tobacco!
He'll stay up and puff his pipe all night.
Whenever there's a crisp spring morning,
when the wind has washed away the clouds
and left the land so cold and dry,
old ghosts can't resist a visit here,
but we don't risk a wisp or trace.
Sometimes it's so quiet and clear
we step into glimpses of the glory days,

fold into echoes of the wool trade and railroad.
We fade in and out of view on the few
remaining wooden streets. We're guests
blown in by high desert wind,
rustling the hotel's shuttered windows.

Driving Past Medical Springs

Empties pitched into the ditch testify
to remote gravel roads cops don't patrol.
Cody's driving, but he tells you, *steer this thing.*
His truck slides across the snowy
Wallowa-Whitman Forest road.
Reaching behind the seat, he cracks
another beer, then chucks the empty Widmer
out the window with a gesture simulating Christmas cheer,
shouting *ho ho ho* so loud it might echo to the north pole.
He hands you one. You crack yours open, too.
Your mother died in August of this year.
Beer tastes better than it should.
It's late December. Union County's beautiful, icicled
and silver, along Highway 203, its snowdrift-sifting cliffs.
Catherine Creek's so white and winterkissed,
a shining, blinding, gorgeous thing, transparent
serpent, cold lifeblood slicing through a canyon.
Who knew a frozen creek could captivate like this?
How can the artesian well beside it be so sweet and free?
How can it be this lovely, but so cruel
to the sweet drowned kids your wife told you about,
the ones who died young just trying to have fun,
riding inner tubes? Who could resist a frigid, wild ride when
June's dry heat burns these mountains brown?
Why do Cody and I risk so much, so thirsty in this cold?
Why not muster a ruckus, some bold fun
before it all gets old and goes to hell.
Look at this clump of rundown buildings amidst dusty sagebrush,
how it can't again hope to pose as forty-room resort hotel.
Its good old days overflowed with gamblers, miners, cowboys

from Pondosa, but Pondosa smoldered out.
Cody points toward its abandoned store:
My dad worked so hard there half his life
but still, the lumber mill closed. The town burned down.
All the West's recklessness won't return
those we miss most, won't even scare away their ghosts.
The Nez Perce never stop to rest here anymore.
Nor do Dunham and Artemisia Wright.
What remains here withered long ago, baked by the high valley,
an Olympic swimming pool not open to the public,
a sun-bleached relic folks drive by and dream they will reclaim.
Something best seen in a black and white photo.
Something in the land they may one day rename.

Joe Bush, Phantom Dredgemaster, Spirits You Away: Sumpter, Oregon

Past the cattle skulls in the Gold Post store,
start your Sumpter Dredge self-guided tour.
Lights flicker on and off. Follow wet footprints
unbidden through a hidden iron door
to where twenty iron buckets a minute and a crew
of twenty men are hard at work again. It's 1881.
Green as seaweed, you almost fall into the sluice
but I rescue you from the box by my metal hand
wired to its arm of whirring gearwheels—
the original digits and limb a dim memory,
crushed back when I was a mechanic.
I shake your hand as gears on dredge and arm spin in sync.
"Hello. I'm Joe. I've redesigned over a hundred feet
worth of machine: we needed a steamship
that could be a Nautilus-like submarine
capable of timetravel, made of dreams,
that tore spud and deadmen from the ground.
We're chasing a giant mechanical fish,"
I cry above the din. "This fish is the annihilation
of space and time, a feat which endlessly fascinates
human beings. Its rusted hull's the technological sublime.
If this dredge retooled as steamship can hijack it,
we may be able to undo some damage done
by the industrial age." Your gaze spies the splendid beast,
its undulating architectures, part of the horizon,
leaping in the air, transparent, filled with lightning.
There are houses in its fins where people see electricity
for the first time. Countrysides flash past,
reflected in its scales, speed multiplied

by transcontinental railroads. Something akin
to the atomic bomb explodes within those blowholes,
dripping with memories. On its lip sits
the vista above the Hoover Dam,
witnessed for the first time. As the dredge,
dream steamship, nears the fish, somewhere deep
within the belly, you hear the fears, the desperate cries
of dying men, miners shouting on a lost hoist,
hurtling a thousand feet down a shaft.
"It's captain Ahab's *hidden lord and master,*
remorseless emperor who made him do
what in his right mind he'd never dare—
nameless, inscrutable, unearthly things.
What men do that brings disaster.
If we catch that leviathan, prepare to meet
the stare of what's worst within us."

Vanport

A golf course, drag strip, and a raceway can't replace
residents lost to the flood of 1948.
Nameless drowned who may have floated out to sea
can't call the coroner a liar. He counted fifteen dead
to keep things orderly. The HAP had claimed the situation safe.
They won't say they gave us twenty minutes to evacuate.
They won't say their sirens blared too late.
No one writes about the white motorist
who revved his car on Denver Avenue and waved his gun,
the one who swore he'd shoot if black families didn't take
their place behind the whites. Some said
hundreds dead were seen from the air
and inside single buildings there.
Those rumors, unsurprisingly, weren't confirmed.
That corporate landlord who collects our rent,
whose strict rules tried to control our lives,
could care less if we lived or died.
That broken dike represents no oversight.
We're just money he'd already spent.
All wars are like that anyway—
when they're over, no one cares
that the poor man died and labored
for the rich man's lavish ways.
I'm drowned, nameless, and still transient,
but I'm free. No one can tell me what to do.
And I'm not paying rent another day.

A Final Duel Between Big Bill and the Cowboy Detective: Tiger Hotel Lobby, Burke, Idaho

Charles Siringo Fires from the Hip

I had my long drink with the Pinkertons
after a blind phrenologist said I had the head
of a detective. As wiry as I am sly,
tough as a pine knot at 135,
trained for danger on the range,
I whiskey-paid my way into the trust
of lode miners in the Coeur d'Alenes
until they coughed up union secrets.
But my plan almost was a bust.
I had to saw a hole into the floor
and crawl under the boardwalk on my belly
just to escape, beneath the breath of men
who'd shoot me as a traitor.
Lucky to leave Burke alive,
I hid inside the Gem Mine for weeks.
Ladies and gentlemen, nice to meet you.
Hope you don't mind the rifle
by my side. My only friend's
my Old Colt 45. As for my enemies—

Okay, Haywood—I'll concede this, at least:
your backside's far outgrown your britches.
Your spirited miners should be digging ditches.
Your federation couldn't chase off all the scabs,
failed to silence all the snitches.
The U.S. Constitution and I agree all men

are at liberty to pursue their interests.
If your muckers don't care for their wages,
send them to the bullpen. Starvation and no pay
may just straighten them for labor.
Our so-called scabs aren't all bad.
They're trying to provide for wives and kids.
Unlike you and Clarence, Haywood, I'm thin,
but Burke's sole narrow street makes it clear
there'll never be room enough for us both here.
You'll arrive and see me waving from the train.
A good detective always stays one step ahead.
But I've left you a nice signed letter with my sentiments
at the Tiger Hotel desk: *Dear Big Bill,*
you, your dynamiters, and your rabid anarchists
can all go to hell—wish Judge Wood and Jury
had indicted you in Idaho. I wish you were dead.
All my worst, you surly bastard
Most Sincerely, Charlie Siringo

Big Bill Haywood Gets the Last Word

Now wait one minute after that outrageous tirade.
Who'd listen long enough to hear it?
Charlie, what fool would believe your lies?
Hiding and lying's your way of life.
Who'd trust a corporate spy?
You're the reason the Governor of Idaho died.
You're why the miners blew the Frisco mine sky high.
And your President calls me undesirable citizen.
You're a swarthy little sellout of a stool pigeon.
A backstabbing lackey paid for whispering campaigns.
A private little prick flitting from city to city,
like those Pinkertons who sneak

through Butte, Telluride, and Cripple Creek,
playing dirty tricks so rich mine owners get richer.
You sold out my federation miners,
men of my own kind, fighting my fight,
men who'd made these mining camps,
who'd dug every pound of ore that ever rose out of a mine.
Your owners made them work unpaid at gunpoint.
Imprisoned them without trial or hearing
during martial law. Many miners died
in the dead of winter in your filthy bullpen prisons.
Charlie, where are their wives and children
while you cavort on horseback in New Mexico?
Remind me—what justice or right came to light
from your time spying undercover?
You turncoat, the only witness
testifying against men you'd befriended
at their trials like that shameless fake, McParland,
conspiring against the Molly Maguires.
Your brand did more than its share of damage.
Your kind of man seeks any advantage.
Darrow said the spiders and vultures
of Wall Street would cheer if I died.
But I'm alive. In spite of you, the rights
of workers and the eight-hour day will prevail.
You are what ails society. You're sure I sailed
from Russia for revenge, and you're afraid.
Well, some friends rerouted your train to Pendleton
the same way we once surprised a train of scabs.
I'd love to glimpse your smug mug, figuring this one out,
detective. I'm not surprised you ran away.
As the last man standing, I and the I.W.W. beat you.
Title your final autobiography
The Life of another Selfish Fool.

Chief Joseph Visits Joseph The Elder's Grave: Joseph, Oregon

Never sell the bones of your father and mother.
—Tuekakas, to a young Chief Joseph

Father, it is Thunder Rolling Down the Mountains,
your son, honoring your memory in Kahmuenem.
I know. The life we knew is brokendown now.
Sorrow has swallowed us like the lost Wallowa Valley.
I spiral down like I'm drowning
in this sacred lake no longer ours.
There's no home anymore in the snowstorm
whitening those mountains you so loved.
But I kept my promise.
I never could have sold your bones to anyone.

How your fingers flew, stringing the wood and sinew bow
for which we were renowned,
tying scoop nets for the steelhead and eel.
Your hands would find the hidden wild onion when we
    were hungry.
Your mouth first asked its permission for harvest.
Your eyes led your bright-eyed daughter,
Swans Lighting on Water, to the wild strawberry,
sweetening your children's smiles.
Moccasined or bare, your feet leaped
astride the wildest horses. When I was a boy
of thirteen snows, you cleaned my throat with willow,

made your child mindful of the wild other world,
so my wyakin, shimmering animal,
would meet me in the clearing between dream and real.

Now you return in pounding sun,
in gusting winds, on the coldest nights of itsiyiyi cries,
and haunt my mind with what once was,
with what might have been.
I miss your wisdom. So many times I've wished you were still here
for advice as I tried to fight for the life that's rightly ours,
for what was promised us. I want you to know

how many moons we rode through deep snows,
our children shivering in deerskins
as they edged across icy cliff faces of the Bitterroots,
sneaking past army barricades, surviving morning raids,
seeking a world where there'd be dignity and peace again.
We were 200 warriors, 500 women and children.
We dreamed of recreating Imnaha and the Wallowa Valley.
On some occasions, when we escaped
the soldiers, or defeated them when outnumbered,

we felt so free that we took flight:
our men and women rode appaloosas up canyons so steep
our pursuers stopped immediately in disbelief.
A few grew feathers and flew like White Bird,
like the animals who'd ruled the world before human beings.
Wrapped in wind, they escaped, part crane, to Canada.
Bird-Alighting stole the Big Hole howitzer.
When we hid, we became invisible.
Our nations could not be bounded, banned, or trapped,
were never made for white men's maps.

After Shore Crossing and Swan Necklace took revenge
    for Eagle Robe,
the peyewit death-spirits followed us. Yellow Wolf spotted
a lone deceased soldier still standing upright beside the river.
After Fire Body shot him, the dead bugler's music continued.
We were at war with Winter, abandoned by Crow,
always chased by treachery and hatred,
by pale shades of men who prayed
to their god of mercy for the chance to kill us all,
to leave meadows red with our dead warriors,
to starve our children. When we stared forward
there always was much farther to go. So much wind and snow.
Father, I know now why you howled those half-mad songs.
You knew what you saw: the white men's useless laws,
America, a liar's paradise.

I was the only leader left to surrender.
I remembered you. And I stood beside our tribe.
I watched us withdraw to the mountains of the Bear's Paw,
pass in Kansas' diseased rivers, in Oklahoma dust,
our old and young alike, wrapped in blankets.
In the heat, deciding how to try and hide our loved ones' bodies.
Good words will not give me back my children.
What a long train I took to talk to the white father in Washington
about tribal rights. There was no comfort in his stare.
He was staring back at all of us, at all our ancestors,
at Ollokot, Toohoolhoolzote, and Looking Glass.
It was America staring back at all our children.
Never sign away our lives, you told us. It echoes.
Chief Lawyer, who talked too much,
believed white greed, and signed treaties
contrived by thieves to cheat us.

We may not have won, but everyone,
even our children, fought nobly
against the endless blizzard
of long knives and their guns.
Our fathers underground are not ashamed.
My dear father, over the years I've survived much hardship
    and pain,
but there was no greater honor than to be your son.

Pastoral with Bestiary

Dear Sulcata Tortoise

When we pulled over suddenly
and I sprinted to save you
before you crossed the busy highway,
then brought you home in the back of our van,
I had no idea you were destined to attain
a greater weight than mine, and to outlive me.
I didn't know I could fall in love with a bulldozer,
a sub-Saharan African eating machine.
I didn't know the tortoise eye could mystify,
staring straight from the Cretaceous,
that your war helmet would ceaselessly
patrol the yard on stubby legs,
part dinosaur, part toddler, ready to do
combat in your shield, carapace encasing
your back legs like a diaper. I didn't know
the other pets would get out of your way
as if they knew you would one day outgrow them.
I had no idea it could be so positively hypnotic
to assist you as you gorge yourself
on arugula and pumpkin,
to watch you luncheon on tufts
of dandelion and clover,
to see you look up at us
with a face like a child's drawing,
flapping your flipper-like arms when frustrated,
or sighing gently when asleep,
just like a human being.

For the Vanished Herds of Great Plains Buffalo

Old Lady Horse
told how the last great herd appeared
to a Kiowa woman:

gathering water from the creekside,
she sees them rise with the first light,
some wounded over rushing water,
scarred horns in the mists.

Old Lady Horse said,
The calves and their mothers
and the few young males
walked to a mountain
and the face of the mountain opened.

Inside it, the world
was green and fresh again
as it had been when she was a young girl.
The rivers ran clear, not red.
The wild plums were in blossom.

Into this world the buffalo walked,
never to be seen again.

Old Lady Horse,
please tell me you mean all of the tribe,

all of the millions of buffalo killed
are still grazing and galloping there
in that better world
within the mountain.

Horseheaven

What if all the wild horses went to heaven in Oregon
on this ridge named for their celestial ascent,
and shattered the grates
over the abandoned cinnabar mines,
galloping unscathed through the barbed wire
and no trespassing signs,
the missing beams of fabulously leaning cabins,
and their living and dead interbred,
transparent stallions grasping mist-breathed mares,
until life and death no longer mattered,
and dun-gray or red foals glowed like clouds
passing over the sun in the Ochoco mountains,
and these lost descendants of Spanish mustangs
strode like conquistadors,
became famously unable to be tamed,
for no human could ever catch them,
they were so quicksilver fast
we could only glimpse their equine outlines
and they'd disappear at will,
long-maned, outracing
the ridiculous pickup trucks
of the bureau of land management,
their glossy shades fading
into suffocating dust.

The Subtle Art of Smuggling a Young Vietnamese Pot-Bellied Pig to Oregon

To do this stylishly, it's best
if a sensitive intelligentsia
willing to master a secret
and perhaps even semi-divine art
coalesces around you.
Form a daring entourage
who'll raise the pig like slaves
raised the emperor Qua Him Sheng,
that ancient, yet famous megalomaniac
who, it's said, gained immortality
by having his heart removed
by an old man of the mountain.

Master this clandestine discipline
as we did, last summer,
past the sneakiest landlord
in Milwaukee, Wisconsin,
into fine hotels, and out to
the mountains of Oregon,
carrying our one-year-old pig
emperor-style: two men raised ends
of a pet taxi covered with a black bed sheet
like some optical illusion
past bureaucrat, and into luxury,
up flights of stairs, onto elevators,
past inquisitive maids and hotel patrons
whose faces registered confusion.

If you must smuggle a pig,
lift with an air of solemn mystery,
as if you're a pallbearer for a mysterious funeral,
as if the whole world depends upon the delivery
of small hooves to your hotel room.
As if you're helping a lunatic get to the moon
or guiding a prophet's soul to heaven,
do this ceremoniously. Contrive
a pig-smuggling caravan.
Raise suitcases that deflect attention.
Let your nomadic band act as one,
as if pig-smuggling's
a noble, serious vocation,
precisely what everyone should practice,
not just right now, but forever.

Ask the most loquacious conspirator
to question the desk clerk, easing tension,
so the pig may be paraded
in true grandeur through the lobby.
Resist the urge to tell extravagant lies.
Don't insist that you're smuggling fine art
or a shred of immortality.
Folly, however clever, is still folly.
But welcome good luck.
May your pig remain silent
at the right times, like ours.
We made a pact: at the first inopportune grunt
we promised to join in and snort
or roar with such tusked fury we'd frighten,
like a tribe of violent swine
amplified from a primitive era.

If he remains silent, imagine him
smiling all-knowingly within,
beneath his black sheet
like an elephant king, escaping the circus,
or like a school of dolphins,
mischievously smiling,
for pigs resemble elephants
and dolphins at particular angles.
Acknowledge your pig
as the true mastermind of this enterprise.
Due to him, you may feel a degree
of the euphoria you'd feel if you freed
all the pigs from factory farm cruelty,
if you loosed wild boar and rhinoceri
from zoos, if you could sneak
a live mastodon into the Pentagon.

When all is silent, let the hotel room door
click softly behind you. Remove your shoes,
and release your waddling god into luxury.
From his lumbering, cumbersome strut,
you will be able to see the emperor is pleased.
Your pig may nod his head like a sensei
and wag his black bristly tail like a dog.
Give yourself over to the love
his snout shows for leftover watermelon.
Delight in his buddhaesque bliss
and know true wisdom is yours
when he rolls over to show you his belly.

Big Guy's

If Big Guy's Diner, that Newport restaurant,
weren't closed, my wife and I decided,
Levin, our 150-pound potbellied pig,
would lounge inside, seated on a stool,
promising to annihilate a pot pie,
impatiently snorting for his plate of food.

Or maybe, he'd be running the place,
full of business, on hind legs and hooves,
with checkered apron draped
over expansive belly,
a paper hat, and perhaps,
a tight-fitting wife beater t-shirt
displaying the slogan,
one hundred percent badass hog!
bon appetit for the boundless appetite,
he'd bellow, heaping up platefuls
of the Fat Man Special
or three-tiered peanut butter sandwich cakes
for his hungry regulars,
big guys who can never get enough food
to eat anywhere else. Every once in a while
everyone would cheer after he cries,
Only Big Guy's knows what it takes
when a great big guy gets hungry!

Kindness

It's a hard world
for little things.
—MARK LINKOUS

teach your children not to torture insects,
the dalai lama instructs mothers and fathers,

advising us to value all lives, despite the size.
If my unborn child respects life like this,

I hereby promise to feel tall, vow not to view
or belittle her concern as weakness. If my child decides

to bless a spider, or worry over a firefly,
I'll celebrate the gesture. I'll remember

the starling which flew into our windshield in northern Iowa,
my wife's flurried prayer afterward for its survival.

The plastic bag of food she carries for stray animals
when we walk the dog, and her funerals

for aphids as a child, have made me mindful.
Though I'm not sure I believe in God, I'm grateful

for her caring, a rare gift in a world
that seldom grants a graceful exit.

I'm grateful the dying field mouse seemed less afraid,
that panting handful Kaley Anna moved from the hot

Milwaukee sidewalk to the neighboring azaleas' soft shade.

Yokum Ridge

We put our trust in a thin, dusty path
that propelled us uphill, over fallen pines,
to meadows overflowing with wildflowers,
flights of blue sky, until Mt. Hood revealed
its smallest waterfalls. Glaciers crackled.
Alone—the last man we'd passed disappeared
after scattering his brother's ashes off the cliff—
we supposed ourselves close to the heavens.
Our labrador retriever raced between us, laughing
as only dogs can, all wild-legged abandon,
past indian paintbrush, lupine, purple aster.
Light showed things' golden edges, shadowed sides.
Pasqueflower seedheads leaned toward us in the breeze.
The true happiness we'd waited for graced our lives.

Missed Photos

Blue lupine and deadwood spill downhill
to the Cloud Cap Inn, the view alone
well worth the road there,
although potholed and brutal.

As snow melts and recedes,
hillsides of rhododendron lead
to a white flash of foothills
devoured by avalanche lilies.

Little Crater Lake's light hue compared
to Crater Lake's deep blue.
Both blues will make you stare,
leave you hexed.
Recover your senses through an exact
point of reference: use Ramona Falls'
white cataract as the low end
to elucidate your color index.

Below Elowah Falls,
windblown mists splash the face, dripping
from bright yellowgreen lichens hundreds of feet tall.
Nothing matters more than rocks spattered
with whitewater's shifting lightshow.

Missed meeting with a friendly mountain goat.
Dogs barked and German hikers gossiped
on the trail back from Ice Lake.

Sun above valleys of clouds.
Larkspur bruise Horseshoe Ridge blue.
Its blush the orange of Indian Paintbrush,
stunning when embarrassed.

Picking blackberries today in the backyard,
the biggest slugs I've ever seen,
like glistening sleeping bags,
camping in a garden planter.

Mt. Hood on a clear night,
a moonlit white shadow.

Angel's Rest

Since it had been left up to me,
and I'd decided to hike further, as I always do,

we stayed too long on top, staring at the view,
trying to trap Silver Star peak

with the right photo. We had to plod down
the pitchblack bluff, socks soaked through,

without proper shoes, on pummeled slush
just now frozen into ice. Cheap flashlights,

conking out, sharpened the stars. Each hush
brought us closer to small waterfalls. Tall pines rushed

uphill, blowing by in heightened nightwinds.
A little dim moonlight subdued a mountain of blindness.

We fell so many times I worried we'd get hurt.
It felt good to sit inert, let the car heater thaw

numb toes and fingers grown so cold.
We all decided it worthwhile

to glimpse the far off river
gorged on silver white and yellow gold.

Nocturne

A great horned owl hooted under the full moon
from its roost high in a pine or juniper late last night.

The most melancholy sound in nature,
wrote Thoreau. *Maniacal hooting of*
some poor weak relic of mortality
who has left hope behind.

So loud it sounded giant.
Bedroom windows broodingly vibrated.

And I realized the mice outside
were fleeing the deathgrip of a winged tiger,
a bird of prey with a taste for brains
but likely to kill anything the right size,
swooping down on their fears with spearlike talons.

How many unheard sounds of fright
would there be tonight?
How many tiny, reverberating lives,
small beings' pantings and sped-up heartbeats?

All this amplified a fear for my life
and the lives of everything else alive,
and I prayed for a burrow for the marsh shrew,
for the skunk's seclusion, for the porcupine's safe hiding,

and thereafter felt a terror of what else
might be hunting out there, plotting violence,

gun-toting human or gliding mountain lion,
at that late hour with its threatening quiet—

the silence of forever, like the Zuni tried to capture,
stuffing their mouths with owl feathers,
hoping to ambush and slit
their worst enemies' throats.

Stillness making me awaken and pace
the cabin's cold floors, try the doors,
and assure they're bolted, shut tight,
until satisfied dog, cat, and wife
were still alive, safely inside,
away from the night.

Reverie

Sometimes, eons recede
in the gaze of my green-eyed tortoiseshell cat,
and a nubile lineage claws its way into the present:
wintering lynx paw the snow
and huntresses nestle tall grass in the Serengeti.
Because her stare is an ancestry
stretching back to the sabertooth,
a ruthlessly beautiful dream
the earth is having
about the speeding cheetah,
the mountain lion leaping from the pine tree,
I move slowly or not at all.
Nothing should disturb such a dream.
As sunlight turns her eyes to gold
so precise a god should use it for a blowtorch
to spread veins through the living,
it could be I am about to see
exactly what led Egypt
to worship the cat as a deity.
I may be about to find out why myth
attributes to her so many omens, so many lives.
Why the world of her fur, arrayed in shades
of red, black, gray, and tan,
lands adeptly after a leap over the fence.
Her tongue, red, delicate rivulet,
caresses little fangs,
keeping all these secrets.

Paean to the Snake River Grade

Moulting into kingsnake summerskin.
Blood cold as the Missoula Flood.
Your bright red horizon mothered by the venom
of Hells Canyon and the Seven Devils,
heatsensing beast who sends rented sedans like this
swerving over volcanic rivers,
scurrying over sunburnt curves,
gutting out ruts and hairpin turns.
You made us feel alive, though
you're less road than reptile:
shedding miles of Idaho high desert,
basalt clasts and granite batholiths,
sheathed in northeastern Oregon forest,
serpentining past what's left of Paradise,
contrary as you blow past Lost Prairie,
your twists, prized by motorcyclists
roaring through Troy, toying with us,
slithering us down past snakebitten towns
from Lewiston Palouse to Joseph Canyon.
Sliding like rockfall or scree off scalded cliffs.
Surly under wheels, spitting dust up at us.
Broad-headedly rattling Grande Ronde River gravel.
Glaring back beady-eyed from the rearview mirror,
your lime kiln hills slowing us down as if sinking
teeth into our sense of time until it unravels,
flashing sparks of feldspar crystals,
birth scars from a quarter of a century
of highway workers' labor, entablatures of fable.
Striped tail of rippling reptilian scales,
holocrystalline, volcanoclastic,

exalting in searing heat shimmer from asphalt,
resting precipices at our shoulders,
flying past vespertine, big-eared bats
roosting in caves and mineshafts,
slowly opening like a snake's mouth to show us
fangs known as the snowy Wallowas,
asmolder with alpenglow, your open throat
a three hundred feet deep ribbon lake
freshly infested with a Loch Ness monster all your own.
Our wheeltreads hissed when we left your abode.
Your forked tongue flicked us
onto some less spinetingling road.

Ape Cave

Stumbling half the afternoon through a lava tube
discovered by a boy scout troop who admired bigfoot
was humbling. The first spelunkers here rappelled
into the subterranean unknown

via ropes, but we stood upright
on smooth, cool stone once so molten
and red hot it could melt bone.
Vaulted ceilings arched like limitless intelligence
but so much teen graffiti defaced walls
it brought doubts about the legacy
of human beings. What if thoughtless stuff

like what's scrawled here, so much less memorable
than natural stone, remains after we're gone,
two billion opposable thumbs' sum total,
rather than one true human poem?
How to blame a critic who'd conclusively deduce,
lewd creatures less interesting than apes?
Perhaps, left to our first instincts, we're a bore,
dull as these flashlights with bad batteries,
prone to repeat the same mistakes, better left
ignored, like those troglodytes held fast
forevermore by Plato's allegory.
The Lascaux cavemen, after all,
left more profound proof
of our worth seventeen thousand years ago.

We emerged with senses more acute, at least.
And the light of day, bravely arrayed
in waves of color, and in varied, dazzling shades,
kept advancing toward us, as if still hoping
to inspire the entire race.

Progress

For Quinton

They're working on a Saturday across the street
on Mississippi Avenue, blocking our driveway
with heavy machinery and a dump truck,
sawing, pounding through Christmas break
to cram in one more of those skinny houses
which populate North Portland, into a lot no wider
than ten or fifteen feet. Progress, I guess,
stares at us every time we leave the house:
the contractor wants the corner lot we rent.
Yesterday, I saw her roll the blueprints out,
and wondered why—there will be no surprises:
another 300,000 dollar glorified garage
made of waferboard, manufactured, all the same.

Taped on my refrigerator,
my four-year-old nephew's crayon drawing:
an impossibly leaning red house
with blue windows and a purple chimney.
This kid has the right ideas.
His sunshine's *yunyine*
his cat, *Adventure Fluffy*
and his pet frog, *Race Car*.
Perhaps sometime before we die
we need to live less in straight lines
and find whatever it is
he has going on inside
this little lopsided house
that leaves its windows
the same color as the sky.

Life as a Cloud in the Blue Mountains

To spend my days adrift
Like these clouds over Eastern Oregon,
Or sell tickets to their whimsical, slow-motion pillow-fights
With the pines, their aimless mysteries.
To wander down into town and snow on a whim
Or merely shadow the valley, threatening to send
Tendrils of my unpredictability.
To take the strange, dreamlike shape
Of lenticular cloud formations.

To stowaway upon those floating ships of fog
Run aground upon the Blue Mountains
And question their deliquescent captain
Before he vanishes into the hold of an abandoned mine.
To confess my admiration for their unnecessary voyages
And ask him to explain why his vaporous zeppelins
Rearrange shape every second
They stay visible in the sky.

To recline on the twilight horizon
And absorb sunset until transformed
Into night itself. To then open into infinite stars.
To spend whole days composed of softly falling rain
Or be one granule of torrential hail.
To exist as a white island, floating over plateaus,
And tend to fences gentle as the torn edge of cumulus
Like pages ripped from the book of mist,
Diminishing simply to assimilate
Into a background of intoxicating blue.

Ghost Town Odes

Acknowledgments

Grateful acknowledgment is owed to the journals where the following poems appeared:

basalt: "Paean to the Snake River Grade"

Big Muddy: "Why the Badlands Look So Bad," "Greenhorn"

Clackamas Literary Review: "Bridal Veil," "Crater Lake Ode," and "In Praise of Slowing Down"

Cloudbank: "Life as a Cloud in the Blue Mountains"

Dalhousie Review: "Dear Sulcata Tortoise"

Excavating Honesty: An Anthology of Rage and Hope in America: "World Renewal Ceremony"

Grain: "Reverie"

Hawaii Pacific Review: "The Cloud Hour," "Please Don't Pick Up the Papayas"

The Kerf: "What Cheer," "Yokum Ridge," and "Angel's Rest"

Lost Coast Review: "Fueled by a Case of Whiskey and a Stubborn Mule, The Notorious James Long Founds Granite, Oregon," "Tule Lake," and "Disatisfied Tourist Complains: Santa Claus, Arizona"

Manifest West: The Western Weird: "Horseheaven"

Paradise Review: "It's No Eldorado"

Stringtown: "Snows of Cornucopia"

Talking River Review: "Dr. W.T. Phy Tells Why the Hot Lake Hotel is Haunted: Hot Lake, Oregon."

Timberline Review: "Huckleberrying"

Weber: The Contemporary West: "Ballad of the Basque Sheepherder: Shaniko, Oregon," "F. Wallace White Recites his Swindler's Soliloquy: Bourne, Oregon"

Windfall: "Forest Road 1819: Rhododendron, Oregon"

Thanks is due to the research library of The Oregon Historical Society, The University of Oregon Library Special Collections, The University of Idaho Special Collections, The Oregonian, and the following authors: Katrine Barber, Verne Bright, Ed Edmo, Diane L. Goeres-Gardner, Ernie LaPointe, J. Anthony Lukas, R. Gregory Nokes, Miles Potter, Manley Maben, Richard Roth, Robert Utley, Philip Varney, Yellow Wolf, and of course, Lambert Florin, all of whose books served as valuable resources and repositories of history.

Notes

"Bridal Veil" refers to two Oregon ghost towns, Bridal Veil and Palmer, which once coexisted in the Columbia River Gorge near Bridal Falls State Park.

"Mt. Tabor Epithalamium" mentions Emperor Norton, or more properly, Joshua Abraham Norton, a San Francisco native who attained no small fame from his declaration in 1859 that he was "Norton I," the true Emperor of the United States. His eccentric proclamations bolstered his status as a popular figure in San Francisco. Over 30,000 people attended his funeral.

"Snows of Cornucopia" was composed in honor of the ghost town of Cornucopia, some of which still stands beside the Cornucopia Mines operation in the Wallowa Mountains of Northeastern Oregon. Snows of fifteen feet or more were commonplace. The Cornucopia Mines was the sixth largest mining operation in the United States, and the longest running mining operation in Oregon.

"Ballad of a Basque Sheepherder" calls upon four important figures from Basque myth:

The *Basajuan*, a yeti-like wild man of the woods, watches over the forests and all wild creatures. A rural genie, protector of flocks, he shouts warnings to the shepherds before a storm and prevents wolves from approaching. He was the first being to cultivate the earth. Humankind obtained the right to also do so when a man won a bet with the Basajaun. This man stole the seeds that the Basajaun was sowing and he returned to his people to teach them how to produce food.

The *Irelu* is a mysterious subterranean spirit who abducts those who disturb him.

Mari, the female divinity of the ancient Basques, is associated with the red or white ram. She is the lady or gentlewoman who lives in caves which reach to the center of the earth. Although she can take on different forms, she often shows herself as a beautiful woman, and moves from one mountain to the next, crossing the sky like a fireball.

The Gaueko is a male personification of the night and all its dangers. If daylight is the realm of humans and the living, night belongs to the spirits and the dead. Thus the Gaueko, when finding a man awake and out at night, will warn him against performing some tasks outside the household when there is no light, and will urge him to go home quickly and stay there until sunrise. Nothing will happen if this person obeys, but if he or she defies these entreaties, the Gaueko will be angered and punish this human.

The Paulina sheep shooters, vigilante cattle ranchers, slaughtered sheep and blindfolded, threatened, and shot sheepherders during the Oregon Range Wars of the early twentieth century.

"The Deep Creek Yuan Gui Speak Their Grievance" attempts to give collective voice to 34 Chinese Miners victimized by the Deep Creek Massacre in May, 1887, on the Oregon shore of Hells Canyon. No one was ever punished for the crime.

The World Renewal Ceremony is a ritual practiced by four Native American tribes in North America. 250 women, children, and elderly members of the peaceful Wiyok tribe, near what is now Arcata, Calfornia, were massacred in 1850 during such a ritual when their warriors were away gathering materials for the ceremony. No one was ever punished for the crime. The Wiyok held their first World Renewal Ceremony since the massacre in 2014.

Celilo was the oldest continuously inhabited community on the North American continent until 1957, when the falls and nearby settlements were submerged by the construction of The Dalles Dam.

Roosevelt, Idaho, an early twentieth century mining camp and accompanying town, originated in 1902 but was quite suddenly submerged by a flood in 1909. Thistle, Utah, succumbed to a similar fate, as did Graun, Italy, which became Lake Reschensee. The saloon piano of Roosevelt does indeed still make music at Yellow Pine school.

Charles Earl Bowles, or Black Bart, an English gentleman bandit known for his style, politesse, and occasional verse, sometimes left poetry behind after he robbed stagecoaches in Northern California and Southern Oregon in the 1870s and 1880s.

Elmer McCurdy's tale is one of the strangest to grace the annals of the Old West. McCurdy, a bank and train robber killed in a shootout in 1911, continued to travel throughout the country via the sideshow and carnival circuit for the next 65 years after his death.

Tule Lake was a World War II "segregation center" in Northern California, very near the Oregon border. The camp was upgraded to a "maximum security" facility in 1943 and poor, overcrowded conditions prevailed. At one time, Tule Lake imprisoned 18,700 Japanese Americans who authorities considered disruptive or disloyal according to their answers to a confusing and poorly worded "loyalty questionnaire." Children who were born or lived at the camp later became poets, painters, and famous actors. One even became an Olympic Gold Medal Weightlifter.

Crowfoot was Sitting Bull's favorite son, and Bloated Jaw, his favorite horse. One of the Lakota's four virtues was generosity, and on the Wild West Show tours, Sitting Bull was known to often give away his money to the homeless. There is no word for goodbye in Lakota; "Toksa Akhe" roughly translates to "We'll see you again." Iya is a Lakota storm-monster who sometimes appears in the form of an infant.

"Letter to James Isabell" is an actual letter from Jesse Cox addressed to Mr. Isabell in 1865. Thanks are due The University of Oregon Special Collections for granting permission for the letter to appear here.

Though all that remains now is a cemetery, Auburn, Oregon, was once the largest town in Eastern Oregon and was the county seat of Baker County. Henry Griffin was the first to discover gold there.

"The Gang Moves Back To the Hotel" speaks from the perspective of a handful of developmentally disabled elderly free spirits who once resided with the poet, nurse, and former mayor of Shaniko, Sue Ann Morelli. Morelli ran an adult foster home at the Shaniko Hotel, which she at one time owned. The group—Charley Franks, Gene Kent, Melton Sawyer, and Howard Lane, and more—were affectionately known as "The Shaniko Gang." Lewis McArthur, in *Oregon Geographic Names*, tell us that "Bakeoven was named for a clay and stone oven built in 1862 to make bread to sell to miners traveling along a trail from The Dalles to gold mines near Canyon City. The baker was said to have been a trader with a pack train of flour whose horses were driven off in the night by Native Americans."

Wet footprints, opening and closing doors, and flickering lights have led some former visitors to believe the ghost of former dredge mechanic Joe Bush haunts the Sumpter Valley Gold Dredge in Sumpter, Oregon. Italicized material at the poem's close hails from Melville's *Moby Dick*.

Vanport was a hastily constructed city of public housing for workers in the Kaiser Shipyards during the second world war. At its peak, it was the second largest city in Oregon, home to 40,000 people, forty percent of whom were African-American. Vanport residents became homeless in 1948 when a 200-foot section of the dike holding back the Columbia River broke during a flood. Vanport was never rebuilt. Survivors had no choice but to relocate. Authorities reported fifteen residents drowned.

The Tiger Hotel Lobby, in Burke, Idaho, must have been an unusual meeting place. Burke, which sits in a canyon only 300 feet wide, accommodated both the railroad and hotel by routing the local train right through the lobby of the Tiger, where the train made a customary stop. This poem also depicts the perspectives of two adversaries in the Coeur D'Alene Mining Wars of the late nineteenth century.

The wyakin was a spirit Nez Perce children discovered at age 12-13 with the help of an elder guide in the wilderness. After this encounter, the wyakin was said to help them the rest of their life. "Itsiyiyi" means coyote in Nez Perce.

Italicized passages in "For the Vanishing Herds of Great Plains Buffalo" come mostly verbatim from Old Lady Horse's "The Last Buffalo Herd." Her version of this Kiowa tale is available in full detail in *Our Hearts Fell To the Ground: Plains Indian Views of How the West Was Lost.*

"Horseheaven" is the name of a ghost town in Jefferson County, Oregon, located near a mostly abandoned forty-acre cinnabar mining operation.

"Yokum Ridge" refers to a trail in the Mt. Hood National Forest. "Angel's Rest" was inspired by an ill-equipped winter hike of the trailhead of the same name in the Columbia River Gorge. A summer hike through the Ape Cave lava tube cavern in Mt. St. Helens State Park inspired "Ape Cave."

"Paean to the Snake River Grade" is an attempt to pay homage to the twists and turns of Oregon State Highway 3 and the landscape this highway introduces to travelers.

About the Author

Matt Schumacher, a former graduate of the Iowa Writer's Workshop, University of Maine Poetry and Poetics Program and the University of Wisconsin–Milwaukee Ph.D. Program in English, serves as poetry editor for the journal *Phantom Drift*, and lives in Portland, Oregon. His other poetry collections include *Spilling the Moon, The Fire Diaries,* and *favorite maritime drinking songs of the miraculous alcoholics.*

redbat
books

For other titles available from redbat books, please visit:
www.redbatbooks.com

Also available through Ingram, Amazon.com,
Barnesandnoble.com, Powells.com and by special order
through your local bookstore.